IGNA

DISCERNMENT of SPIRITS

in Spiritual Direction and Pastoral Care

Other Books by Mark E. Thibodeaux, SJ

God's Voice Within

Reimagining the Ignatian Examen

IGNATIAN
DISCERNMENT *of* SPIRITS
in Spiritual Direction and Pastoral Care

GOING DEEPER

MARK E. THIBODEAUX, SJ

LOYOLA PRESS.
A JESUIT MINISTRY
Chicago

LOYOLA PRESS.
A JESUIT MINISTRY

3441 N. Ashland Avenue
Chicago, Illinois 60657
(800) 621-1008
www.loyolapress.com

Cover art credit: Galina Timofeeva/iStock/Getty Images

ISBN: 978-0-8294-4958-7
Library of Congress Control Number: 2020934250

Printed in the United States of America.
20 21 22 23 24 25 26 27 28 29 Bang 10 9 8 7 6 5 4 3 2 1

Contents

Introduction: Building on the Foundations of the Rules for Discernment

This book is intended to be a helpful resource for spiritual directors and pastoral counselors of the Catholic Church, be they laypeople, religious sisters or brothers, or priests. The book presumes that you have some training in this field and that you are already more than familiar with St. Ignatius's Rules for Discernment of Spirits. If you have not already done so, I recommend that you spend some time with that primary text, which can be found among the appendixes of St. Ignatius's *Spiritual Exercises*, and also that you read one or two books delving into the subject on an introductory level.[1]

This book is a humble attempt to build on the brilliant foundations of St. Ignatius's ideas. It is meant to get us pondering the contemporary applications of this classic text. How might we use the Rules for Discernment in our work as directors and counselors? What new insights do we glean from the spiritual and intellectual growth of the past nearly half millennium since Ignatius first penned the work?

After briefly presenting a "refresher" on the basics of the Rules for Discernment, the book builds on the foundations of the Rules in two ways. First, I present twelve "experimental" ideas about discernment of spirits. I call them "experimental" because they are not part of the original work but rather are ideas that have evolved in my own practice of employing the Rules in my work as spiritual director and pastoral counselor. They are experimental because they have not yet passed the scrutinizing test of time, nor have they been "endorsed" by any authoritative body.[2] Instead, they are musings—nuggets I have panned out of the gold-laden rivers of years of spiritual conversations. You may find that many of these nuggets will indeed have a bit of gold in them, but some may melt away in the fire of implementation. Although I can't say that every one of the experimental ideas will prove to be helpful through and through, I can assert that they point to realities that you will encounter again and again in your work as director or counselor.

The second way that I build on the foundations is by exploring how our employment of the Rules for Discernment of Spirits might affect our work as directors and counselors. Specifically, how do we treat differently a directee or counselee who is in consolation versus one who is in desolation, false consolation, and so on? St. Ignatius has wonderful tips upon which I attempt to build.

A Crash Course in Ignatian Discernment of Spirits

In this section, I present a "travel pack" of information on Ignatian discernment. I cover just the basics.

Ignatian Discernment: What Is It?

Practically every minute of our waking day, we are making decisions: most of them really small, and some of them far reaching. We know that even the small decisions add up to define who we are and what we are doing with our lives. The problem is that we tend not to take the time and trouble to discern our paths. Instead, we let circumstance and our unconscious emotions (especially our fears and desires) decide for us. All of us are guilty of DUI, so to speak—we are driving under the influence of movements within us of which we are hardly even aware.

This is the genius of St. Ignatius: he knew that God can be found in all things, but he also knew that we cannot find God in every decision unless we consciously seek God out. Thus, Ignatius challenges us to explore the movements within us that are leading us to lean one way or another. I know that I'm drawn to option B, but why? What movement inside of me draws me that way? If I don't take the time to ponder that question, I may well choose option B for all the wrong reasons.

Inside all of us is a movement away from God and God's plan. There is also a movement toward God and God's plan. Ignatius calls the inner pull away from God "the evil spirit," whereas he calls the inner pull toward God "the good spirit." Our task in discernment, then, is to determine whether it is the evil spirit or the good spirit that is drawing us toward one option and away from another.

How Do We Identify the Various States of Being?

When we are in a mood of listening to the evil spirit—when we are "driving under the influence" of the evil spirit—Ignatius says that we're in desolation. Today, when we say, "I'm in a bad space right now," we often mean that the evil spirit has gotten hold of us and we're struggling not to follow it. When we are in a mood of listening to the good spirit—Ignatius calls this con-solation—we say, "I'm in a good space." Sometimes when we are in desolation, we are well aware of it, but other times we're convinced that we're in good space—that we're doing the right thing—when in fact we are moving away from faith, hope, and love. In these situations, the evil spirit has played a double trick on us: it has drawn us away from God's plan for us, and it has also convinced us that we are on the right path. This state of self-deception is what Ignatius calls false consolation.

And so, we ask ourselves, "Which spirit is moving me? What is my spiritual state of being—my spiritual 'mood'? Am I in consolation? Desolation? Or false consolation? How can I tell?" Obviously, it is not always easy to know what state of being we are in at any given moment. There is no foolproof way of knowing, but we can look out for a few signs that might indicate the state of being in which we find ourselves.

Detecting Consolation

Among the telltale signs of consolation, two stand out as most important:

- **Being "in sync" with God and God's action in the world.** Do you have a strong sense of God's presence in your life at this moment? Do you have a sense of God's will for you, and does it come fairly naturally for you to do God's will? Do you feel as though God and you are in a groove together? Does it feel as if God and you are dance partners and no one is stepping on toes? Do the wise people in your life who know you well also believe that you're tapping into God's will and following God's lead at this moment? (This last question helps prevent false consolation.)

- **Having great desires for faith, hope, and love.** Do you sense in your heart a strong desire to do the most loving thing possible in this situation? Do you have genuine care for the people you live and work with, including the difficult people? Are you hopeful and faithful? Are you optimistic? Do you have a sense that God is going to help you sort everything out and that it'll turn out fine in the long run? Do the wise people who know you well also believe you are acting out of sincere faith, hope, and love? (Again, this last question helps prevent false consolation.)

Here are other characteristics of a person in consolation:

- **Experiencing peace and tranquility.** In consolation, you may well be experiencing turmoil, anxiety, or stress on the *surface*, but even in the midst of the emotional challenges of your life, there is a *deep down* tranquility—a sense that God is present and that all will be well. Consider the famous words of Psalm 23:

Even though I walk through the valley of the shadow of death, I will fear no evil, for you are with me; your rod and your staff comfort me.

Note that the psalmist is on a terrible journey . . . valley (bad!) . . . shadow (worse!) . . . death (worst of all!). On the surface, it is an emotionally trying time. But deeper down, the psalmist is comforted, knowing that God is near. "I fear no evil, for you are with me." The psalmist, despite being in a valley, is in consolation.

- **Being transparent with the director and with trusted loved ones.** In consolation, you are naturally more inclined to be open about your behaviors and your inner life. Even if you're a bit embarrassed about some things, your peace and tranquility give you the courage to say what you need to say to those you trust. And your desires for faith, hope, and love lead you to pursue spiritual growth, even at the expense of embarrassing yourself.

Detecting Desolation

Ignatius tells us that desolation is simply the opposite of consolation.[3] Therefore, the telltale signs of desolation are the opposite of those described above.

- **Being "out of sync" with God and God's actions in the world.** You are in desolation when you don't have a strong sense of God's presence in your life. It isn't necessarily a crisis in faith—you aren't doubting the existence of God. But you just can't seem to feel God's presence. It feels as though God is distant. Wise people in your life are telling you that you seem "out of sorts" or that "you are not yourself lately."

- **Having a lack of desire for faith, hope, and love.** You feel unmotivated to do the right thing. Maybe you're still more or less behaving like a good Christian, but interiorly it feels as though you're just "going through the motions." You feel spiritually lethargic, depleted, apathetic.

- **Experiencing disquiet, fear, inner disturbance.** When you are in consolation, you may well be feeling emotionally challenged—in a valley of the shadow of death—but deeper down, you are at peace. In desolation, you feel a deep-down disquiet, regardless of how things are going in your exterior life. You feel deeply anxious, upset, alone, or threatened. Or maybe you just feel surly, crabby, or cranky.

- **Lacking transparency.** When in desolation, you are guarded, unforthcoming, closed—even with those you love and trust. You are less willing to open your heart to your director or to your loved ones. You find yourself dodging questions and avoiding vulnerable conversations.

Detecting False Consolation

The trickiest state of being to recognize is, of course, false consolation. It's tricky because on the surface it looks and feels like consolation. Your actions and inclinations *seem* loving and hopeful. You *feel* like you are in sync with God. So how would you discover the "serpent's tail"?—as St. Ignatius once called it.[4] These are a few telltale signs (pardon the pun):

- **A very subtle rebelliousness.** You are a tiny bit cheeky with the people around you. You are not quite as open to constructive criticism or to exploring the possibility that you are being misled at the moment. You might start to act in subtly rebellious ways—a rebelliousness that you yourself do not pick up on.

- **Secrecy, or at least a lack of transparency.** You are not as forthcoming with your account of all that's going on in your life—your emotions, reasonings, and behaviors. You might even avoid coming to see your director or consulting your spouse. This, as opposed to a person in consolation, who might say, "I really want to keep this to myself, but I probably should tell you everything. So here goes . . .," or "I feel strongly that I am doing the right thing, but I want to know what you think about it."

- **A reversal of past good decisions.** For the most part, subsequent good decisions will be a progression from past good decisions. God will not capriciously lead you from one direction to another. God leads you on a discernible trajectory. Sometimes false consolation can be determined by the unusual reversal of course that you seem to be making.

- **A false urgency.** A person in false consolation often feels compelled to act dramatically and quickly despite the fact that the wise and loving people in your life believe there is no rush and that it would be better to spend more time discerning before acting. You lack Ignatian indifference—the spiritual freedom—either to act on this immediately or to hold off for a while, as opposed to a person in true consolation, who might say, "I feel intensely drawn to this right now, but I don't need to rush. I can pray and deliberate a while more if need be." As already stated, the person in false consolation who does not receive affirmative reactions from trusted advisers and loved ones might then start to act in subtly rebellious ways.

Once we have identified the state of being, what should we do next?

When you are in *consolation*, you have "the good spirit as your counselor," so you can trust your spiritual instincts. Because you are in sync with God, you can move in the direction you feel inclined. If you feel it best to wait and discern some more, you can trust that instinct, too.

Desolation, however, is trickier. Ignatius says that a person in desolation has "the evil spirit as his counselor." So you can't trust your gut. You're going to have to use your instruments to fly the plane rather than rely on your own perceptions. Here are five things you should do:

- **Name the desolation** and articulate its characteristics. Half the battle is won when you have correctly diagnosed the problem.
- **Avoid making important decisions or sweeping judgments** about yourself, other people, or about your present situation.
- **Lean more heavily on your support network.** Visit your "elders" more frequently. Consult your spouse or good

friend. Seek out professional help through books, counselors, and the like.

- **Be firm with the evil spirit.** Don't allow yourself to engage in unhealthy or sinful behaviors. Don't "check out" of life-affirming activities. Force yourself to think and act out of hope and optimism, even if you don't feel very hopeful or optimistic. Do not let your prayer routines slip. If anything, increase them a little bit in order to spiritually fortify yourself. (But only a bit. Otherwise you might experience burnout, which will only make matters worse.)

- **But be gentle on yourself.** Meanwhile, don't think harshly of yourself and don't beat yourself up for mistakes or for feeling low. Treat yourself to some wholesome and enjoyable activities like going for a hike, listening to good music, or watching an uplifting movie.

As already stated, *false consolation* is the trickiest state of all. If you're truly in false consolation, you won't know it, so you won't follow my or anyone else's advice! I'll say only this: If you have loved ones who are wise and reliable, why don't you trust them when they are warning you that you might be deceiving yourself? Do you really think that you're above self-deception? Why not consider the possibility that you've taken a wrong turn and haven't noticed? Take a sober and honest look at yourself, pondering the telltale characteristics of false consolation that are stated above. Play the devil's advocate by building a case against your supposed consolation. Might your loved ones be right? If you begin to suspect that you have been in false consolation, then treat it as the desolation that it is. Follow the five instructions above.

Notes

_____

_____

_____

_____

_____

_____

_____

_____

_____

_____

_____

_____

_____

_____

_____

_____

_____

_____

Notes

PART ONE

TWELVE INNOVATIVE IDEAS ABOUT DISCERNMENT OF SPIRITS

Building on the Foundations of Ignatius's Ideas

There exist among us fans of Ignatius a resistance to adapting and building on the Rules for Discernment of Spirits. We are too afraid of tampering with the work of our "Master Ignatius." But the early Society of Jesus promoted such innovation. In the years before and after Ignatius's death, new commentaries—called "directories"—on the Exercises arose. Some of the instructions found therein stretched Ignatius's original ideas quite a bit. As opposed to Ignatius's vision of one-on-one direction, one directory recommends a sort of group-sharing among the retreatants.[5] As opposed to Ignatius's strict instructions about praying "the full hour,"[6] another directory recommends that retreatants pray less than a full hour if they are not spiritually mature.[7] Still another recommends that a retreatant be given, in addition to a retreat director, an evening conversation partner "for suitable recreation"![8]

If we are to keep the Rules alive, we must not only employ them; we must also build upon them, using insights from theology, science, psychology, and spirituality that were not yet in existence when Ignatius wrote the Rules. To use only one example, how might our contemporary knowledge of the psychological conditions of depression and mania have an impact on how we understand desolation and false consolation? We must explore questions such as these if we want the Rules to live on.

What follows are twelve innovative ideas regarding Ignatian discernment. Some of them have big implications and require a bit of explanation. Others are small but relevant observations that can be presented in only a few sentences. These experimental ideas spring not from academic research but rather from my personal experiences of explicitly employing the Rules for Discernment for more than ten years with my directees, my novices, and in my own spiritual life. By calling these ideas "experimental" I am humbly admitting that one or another of them might be wrong—or at least in need of some tweaking. And so I present them to you in the hope that you will experiment with them in your own ministry and spiritual life. If they turn out to be both true and helpful, we'll come to know that by their effectiveness in the vineyard of the Lord.

So here goes . . .

1

Idea #1: False Spirit Is a More Effective Term Than Evil Spirit

In today's multicultural society, the term *evil spirit* can lead to distracting misunderstandings. People from more traditional cultures will begin to imagine some sort of demonic possession. Meanwhile, many in today's world will be turned off by the notion of a little pitchforked red devil coming after us. In both situations, I find myself as a director having to engage in distracting theological conversations at the very moment when my desolate directee is sensitive and unable to explore challenging theologies.[9]

If I use the term *false spirit* and define it as any movement within myself that leads me away from God and away from faith, hope, and love, practically everyone can get on board with that term.

I also like to call the false spirit "false" because much of the work of spiritual direction is uncovering the lies or—even more frequently—the twisted truths upon which my directee has subconsciously operated as he or she negotiates a difficult aspect of life. Ignatius says that the false spirit brings "fallacious reasonings, subtleties, and continual deceptions."[10] If I think the directee is able to handle it, I like asking the question, "What are the lies the false spirit is telling you as you try to work through this disagreement with your spouse?" If someone is in deep desolation, I sometimes even have directees write down in a journal every lie or twisted truth that the false spirit is shouting in their ear and also, on a separate list, what truths the good spirit is whispering.

The former English teacher in me is bothered by the parallelism problem of using *false* versus *good* spirit instead of *false* versus *true* spirit, but I simply don't believe that *true spirit* is an apt descriptor of the good spirit. So I've decided to make my peace with the inconsistency.

Notes

_____

_____

_____

_____

_____

_____

_____

_____

_____

_____

_____

_____

_____

_____

_____

_____

_____

_____

Notes

2

Idea #2: There Are Three Uses for the Rules for Discernment: Large, Short, and Situational Movements

Ignatian practitioners usually use the vocabulary of *desolation* and *consolation* to describe big, sweeping movements of one's interior life—movements lasting years, or at least months. For example, someone might say, "My college years were a time of consolation for me," or "My adolescence was a long period of desolation for me." A priest might say, "The six years I was assigned to St. Ignatius Parish was a period of desolation," and a layperson might say, "Our early years of married life were filled with consolation."

However, we need not limit this valuable vocabulary to describing only one's long-term states of being. For example, we can also use this vocabulary to describe smaller movements within those large ones. Isn't it true that while I might be in an overall state of consolation at this phase of my life, I might also have my fair share of brief moments of desolation in the midst of that general state of consolation? If the distinction between desolation and consolation is being in sync with God's presence and having great desires for faith, hope, and love, then might we say that a given person could be *generally* in consolation at this time of her life but that in this particular week she has slipped into a mild sadness that, in turn, has made her less aware of God's presence and less inclined toward faith, hope, and love? The reverse could also be true: she is in a spiritually dark period of her life but is having a little bit better week this week wherein she has a better prayer experience and is feeling a bit more hopeful about life.

Could we stretch this idea a little further? Regardless of my *general* state of consolation, might I have momentary spiritual lapses wherein I'm in a foul mood and am grumpily snapping at people? Perhaps I didn't sleep well last night and I'm grumpy throughout the morning. Then, during my lunch break, I pray my Ignatian Examen and begin to channel God's presence a bit better. By the time I get back to the office, I feel better and have become a decent person to work with again. Indeed, this is the very purpose of the twice-daily Examen: to name my spiritual state of being this half day and, with God's help, to make any course corrections to be more faithful, hopeful, and loving in the next half day.

Ignatius himself is quite versatile in his use of this vocabulary of *consolation* and *desolation*. He doesn't restrict himself to one setting for the use of this valuable tool but rather uses it in different ways. For example, Ignatius tells us that we should not make a decision while in desolation. But when he speaks about "three times when we make a decision," he says that the second time is when "light and understanding are derived through experience of desolations and consolations."[11] Isn't he contradicting himself here? Shouldn't we be in consolation (only) when making a decision? Ignatius is using this vocabulary in two different ways simultaneously. He is presuming that you are in a *general* state of consolation when discerning your choice, but that while praying about the different scenarios in your prayer time—what I call "praydreaming"—you notice whether your heart and soul feel consoled or desolate as you praydream each choice.

Thus, one could use this Ignatian vocabulary to describe at least two simultaneous states within oneself: a general state of being and a moment-by-moment state of being. I often use the ocean as a metaphor to describe this. In the ocean there are always little surface-level ups and downs (moment-by-moment desolation or consolation) while at the same time deep below there are the more significant tides moving the whole ocean one way or the other (longer-term desolation or consolation).

The distinction we've been using thus far has been about duration: a long-term state of being (months and years) versus a short-term state of being (moments, hours, or maybe a day or so). But let us leave duration for a moment. Might there be other ways in which we could use this vocabulary? What about situational consolation or desolation, wherein a certain *situation* leads me naturally toward one state or another? Some examples:

- Every time I talk politics with my sister, my blood boils.
- My great friend Tom brings the best out of me.
- Everything at work is going fine, but lately things are not going well at home. Whenever I'm with the family at

home, I get grumpy and snap at everyone. I don't feel God's presence inside me when I'm around my family these days.

- As a Jesuit high school teacher, I'm experiencing God's presence and great desires in my work but feeling desolation in my community. Or perhaps, to complicate things, I am in consolation while in the classroom with my students but in desolation while working with my department chair.

These are examples of what I call situational consolation or desolation. The state of being is brought about not by a time of day but by the situation. Looking at the first example, I might have a spiritual directee who is generally in consolation but finds himself in a state of desolation when discussing politics with his sister. As his director, I could help him see the characteristics of consolation in his overall way of being. We could talk about how to make the most of it. But I could also help him see that, when speaking with his sister, he is in a state of desolation and that he should—when interacting with his sister—follow Ignatius's sound advice regarding desolation. For example, he should not make any rash decisions ("I'm just going to stop visiting her"). He should pray before approaching her house. He should ask God especially for hope and love whenever she brings up politics.

Notes

_____

_____

_____

_____

_____

_____

_____

_____

_____

_____

_____

_____

_____

_____

_____

_____

_____

Notes

3

Idea #3: We Can Apply These States of Being to Organizations, Groups, and Relationships

We tend to limit our use of discernment of spirits to the state of being of an individual person, but might we also use this tool when reflecting on the state of being of organizations? For example, might a church parish or a Catholic high school be in a state of consolation or desolation? From there we could break it down even further. Perhaps the parish youth group is unknowingly experiencing false consolation while the parish council is in consolation. Perhaps the Catholic high school on the whole is in consolation, but the athletic department is in desolation.

Might we teach families to reflect on their state of being as a family? Is the family—as a unified body—growing in their desires to act as a family of faith, hope, and love? Is the family growing closer to or farther away from God? What about a married or dating couple? Might they, too, go through stages of desolation and consolation? Might it help them to reflect on their relationship in this way? I wonder if we might reflect on the stages of growth in a dating relationship through the lens of discernment of spirits. For example, isn't infatuation simply one form of false consolation? If so, what insights might the Rules for Discernment of Spirits provide that could aid us in accompanying a person who is infatuated?

Isn't it true that ordinary friendships go through stages of consolation and desolation? What about a local Jesuit community? A province? Might the global Society of Jesus go through these various states? How about the Roman Catholic Church? Or the presbyterate of a diocese? How about a city? A region? Or even a nation?

On this last point about a nation going through the various stages, might this be a unique contribution that Ignatian practitioners could bring to the public discourse? Might we share the insights of Ignatius and then ask voters to reflect on their motives for voting for one candidate or another? Are their motives grounded in faith, hope, and love? In fear? In greed? Are we voting from a place of desolation? Consolation? False consolation? Might we share these insights with those in public office as well?

Notes

Notes

4

Idea #4: The Distinction between a Spiritual State of Being and an Emotional One Is Important, but Not Too Important

Many have rightly pointed out that not all consolations and desolations are spiritual.[12]

For example, one might experience emotional desolation in the midst of spiritual consolation. That is, one might experience sadness, anger, lethargy, and so on, but still have a strong sense of God's presence and still have a strong desire for faith, hope, and love. This is an important distinction. My predecessor in the novice director job, Billy Huete, SJ, used to say, "We treat spiritual problems with spiritual remedies, but we treat psychological problems with psychological remedies." For example, a person with depression caused by a chemical imbalance in the brain needs medical treatment and should not simply try to "pray through" the problem. This is why the distinction between spiritual and emotional states of being is important.

However, in my experience, *for the most part*, the method of diagnosis and the treatment for both spiritual and emotional desolation is the same. If a person is in spiritual desolation, she should avoid making major life decisions. She should be firm with the false spirit but gentle with herself. She should actively pursue the virtue of hope. But what if she is in *emotional* desolation—some sort of mild depression, for example? How would her director's advice change? Looking back over the "treatment" for spiritual desolation—no major decisions, be firm with the false spirit, be gentle on yourself, have hope—would any of these treatments be detrimental to a person in emotional desolation rather than spiritual desolation? Indeed not. The treatment is mostly the same.

Notes

Notes

5

Idea #5: Consolation, Ignatian Indifference, and Spiritual Freedom Mostly Refer to the Same Phenomenon

For a while now, I have been operating under the assumption that the following terms mean almost the same thing. I use the "approximately equal" sign to indicate this:

Consolation	≈	Ignatian Indifference	≈	Spiritual freedom

And this:

Desolation	≈	Disordered attachments	≈	Spiritual unfreedom(s)

I say approximately equal because we could easily come up with some slight distinctions among them. However, they are equal enough to treat them all the same way when working with directees or with our own spiritual lives. For example, if I am in desolation, I will avoid making decisions or judgments. I would do the same regarding disordered attachments and spiritual unfreedoms. Just above I said that while there is a difference between a spiritual state of being and an emotional one, the method of diagnosis and treatment is mostly the same. Here I'm suggesting that the same could be said when we find ourselves using, for example, the words *indifference* and *consolation*. While there may be a distinction between these words in theory, they end up being virtually the same in practice.

Notes

Notes

6

Idea #6: There's Such a State as Difficult Consolation

All of us are rightly wary of the incorrect reduction of the concepts of desolation and consolation to merely feeling bad and feeling good. But the reason this misconception is so persistent is that we do indeed *usually* feel good in consolation and *usually* feel bad in desolation. It's an understandable mistake, then, to reduce such states to those feelings. We are not helped by the *Autobiography* when St. Ignatius seems to reduce the states to "sad" and "joyful."[13] In that spot in the autobiography, Ignatius is showing us how simple was his own understanding of these states *as he began* the spiritual life. Note that as a beginner in the spiritual life, he had no notion of false consolation. In his Rules for Discernment of Spirits he delves into the subtleties of the spiritual life and no longer reduces the states to "sad" and "joyful." He now has a name for the experience of *feeling* consoled while unknowingly *being* in the state of desolation. He calls this state false consolation and rightly explains that it is, in fact, desolation. With this third state, we can put together a matrix:

Figure 1

	Actually Is Consolation	**Actually Is Desolation**
Feels like consolation	Consolation	False Consolation
Feels like desolation	?	Desolation

When it feels like consolation and it actually is, Ignatius calls it consolation. Likewise, when it feels like desolation and actually is, he calls it desolation. He then adds nuance by giving the name *false consolation* to the state in which it feels like consolation but actually is desolation. But the matrix exposes a lacuna. What might we call the state in which it feels like desolation but actually is consolation? Ignatius has no name for this. Instead he lumps the experience in with "regular" consolation, saying that consolation can be accompanied by tears of sorrow or of joy.[14]

Not having a name for this experience is a problem because it is an incredibly common occurrence. To name just a few examples, we might experience grief, psychological depression, righteous anger, and fear, yet still be in sync with God and have great desires for faith, hope, and love. We might be suffering from unrequited love or from dry prayer. We might—despite our best efforts—have failed at something important to us and are terribly sad about it. These kinds of experiences happen to us all the time. We need a name for it if we're going to be using this language regularly in pastoral counseling, spiritual direction, and so on. For the past several years, then, I have been using the term *difficult consolation* to refer to this spiritual state of being. The people to whom I've introduced this term—such as spiritual directees and novices—have found it tremendously helpful, as have I as their director.

We have learned that St. Teresa of Calcutta had terrible interior struggles for decades. The experience is painfully laid out in the posthumously published memoir *Come Be My Light*. When giving workshops on discernment of spirits, I am often asked about her situation. It is indeed a puzzling case. How could someone who was so in sync with God and who so obviously passionately pursued faith, hope, and love be considered to be in desolation all that time? It seems to me that as we traditionally think of consolation and desolation, Mother Teresa simply doesn't fit the categories. However, she could be the patron saint of those in difficult consolation. She fits the description perfectly: she was in fact in consolation. We know this by her unquestionable sanctity and love for humankind. But she was also miserable, and she interiorly experienced the *feelings* of desolation. She was in difficult consolation. The same might be said of St. John of the Cross's experience of the "dark night of the soul."

Notes

Notes

_____

_____

_____

_____

_____

_____

_____

_____

_____

_____

_____

_____

_____

_____

_____

_____

_____

_____

_____

_____

7

Idea #7: Often, the Path from Desolation to Consolation Passes through Difficult Consolation

Now let's have a little fun with this matrix. When we are in desolation, we want badly to move to consolation (duh!). The problem is that, rather than allowing God to take us there at God's own slow pace, we impatiently try to force our way there on our own. This leads to disaster because not allowing the Lord to lead us is, by definition, desolation. We will never get to the promised land of consolation by this path. Instead, we will find ourselves in a self-manufactured consolation, which of course is just another type of desolation. If you will, the arrow of our heart, aiming for consolation, ricochets off an impenetrable wall and lands us in false consolation.

The sad truth of the matter is that usually there is no direct trip from desolation to joy-filled consolation. Instead, we must allow the Lord to carry us on a long and arduous journey through difficult consolation. We must spend a while there, and then, when we have received the hard graces that come only from difficult consolation (such as the best of them: humility), the Lord will carry us to the state of joyful consolation.

Figure 2

	Actually Is Consolation	**Actually Is Desolation**
Feels like consolation	Consolation	False consolation
Feels like desolation	↑ Difficult consolation	← Desolation

What is the point of all this silly talk of arrows and ricochets? Unfortunately, this phenomenon is all too common in our spiritual life and in the life of the people to whom we minister. A couple of examples:

- A woman is unhappy in her marriage but afraid to confront her husband. After months of emotional agony, she decides to become a full-time volunteer at the Jesuit church parish. She "happens to" volunteer for time blocks in which her husband is home from work. Sadly, this also is the time when her lonely daughter returns home from school. The wife falls in love with her church work in an almost manic way. Now, a beginner in the spiritual life might think that a drive to do more church work couldn't possibly be from the false spirit. But we know better. Let us say that, as is often the case, the move toward love would involve confronting the husband and working through the fallout. The Lord is calling her to this painful act of love. If she were to answer that call, she probably would spend time in the desert land of difficult consolation. We call it difficult for obvious reasons: it would be painful in many ways. We call it consolation because she would be in sync with God and would be practicing love, albeit "tough love." Instead, she tries to find her *own* path to consolation. She manufactures a "holier" life in which she spends much more time at church, to the detriment of her vocations to married life and parenting. She is in false consolation.

- A Jesuit has been teaching sophomore English in the same school for many years. His only friend in the community has just been transferred. He is lonely and bored. In the middle of one sleepless night, he gets an idea for a new ministry to the moms of the students. He'll start a mothers' support group! He pitches the idea both to his superior and to the principal. Both are skeptical, but they do not stop him. Over the course of the year, he founds and facilitates an intensely active group. Over time, he begins to neglect his classes. Having less time for grading, he gives fewer writing assignments and no longer turns in his grades on time. Because the group meets in the evenings, he misses most community suppers nowadays. Furthermore, he begins to fall for a young mom in a rocky marriage who has confided in him. Danger! Danger! As in the above example, we have a person who has tried to force his way out of the legitimate suffering of difficult consolation (for example, by prayerfully grieving the loss of a good friend) and has as a result found himself doing something that makes him feel better but isn't actually what God is calling him to.

Notes

Notes

_____

_____

_____

_____

_____

_____

_____

_____

_____

_____

_____

_____

_____

_____

_____

_____

_____

8

Idea #8: Is Your State of Being Placid or Dramatic?

After successfully diagnosing the spiritual state of being of myself or of a directee, it is helpful to determine the *intensity* of the experience. Why? Because the experience of intense desolation is quite different from the experience of a more low-grade-fever sort of desolation. The same is true of all the other states as well.

One might experience a state of being as placid or dramatic. What might that look like for each state?

- **Dramatic consolation.** I am overwhelmed with joy. I feel deep love for everyone, and I'm inspired toward acts of kindness and generosity. I sense deeply the love that God has for me—and it leaves me humble and in awe. I am left wondering, "Can life really be this good? Can God really be this good? Yes, indeed!"

  - Biblical images:

    - Mary: "My soul proclaims the greatness of the Lord. My spirit rejoices in God my savior. For He has looked upon his handmaid's lowliness . . . . Holy is His name." (Luke 1:46–49)

- The Israelites dancing and singing, just after crossing the Red Sea: "I will sing to the Lord, for he is gloriously triumphant; horse and chariot he has cast into the sea." (Exodus 15)
- The psalmist, when feeling inspired to say, "What return shall I give to God for all the good that God has done for me? I shall take up the cup of salvation and call upon the name of the Lord." (Psalm 116, paraphrased)

- **Placid consolation.** I am not ecstatic or overwhelmed with joy, but I am at peace and am happy to be alive today. I'm not thrilled about anything (my loved ones, my work), but I am happy to be who I am and more than happy to do the work (spiritual and otherwise) that God seems to be calling me to do. I go about my day peacefully and quietly, trying to be the best person I can be. I am neither on a "high" nor a "low." I am even-keeled.

  ○ Biblical images:

    - Jonathan, who seems content to play second fiddle to David and works quietly to reconcile David with King Saul
    - St. Joseph, happy to do the difficult tasks that God has asked of him. Not needing to be center stage
    - St. John, on whom Jesus counted more than anyone else for emotional support—"the one whom Jesus loved"—and yet almost never does or says anything dramatic or noteworthy

- St. James, who in the book of Acts seems to be the leader of the church, but who does his work without fanfare or controversy

- **Dramatic desolation.** I am in despair. I feel absolutely miserable or fearful, or full of rage, or hopeless. I feel tempted to draw rash negative conclusions about my relationships, my work, my life. I feel tempted to do something dramatic like abandon my vows, quit my job, or tell off my partner. I cry or brood or yell all the time these days.

  - Biblical images:

    - The Israelites in the desert, wailing and grumbling about the food
    - Judas Iscariot, who in despair and self-loathing kills himself
    - Jonah, who at the end of the story says, "Kill me now"
    - Tobit, when he wrongly accuses his wife of stealing and cruelly excoriates her
    - Martha, who is angry at Mary and is "anxious about many things"

- **Placid desolation.** I feel lethargic. I just don't care about anything. My sin isn't doing something dramatically unloving but rather not doing anything at all—a sin of omission. I am just treading water, doing the bare minimum to keep everybody off my back. I can't be bothered. I am a wet blanket. I check out from life.

  - Biblical images:

- Pilate, who doesn't believe Jesus is guilty of anything but doesn't care enough to do anything about it: "I wash my hands of this."
- The man in the parable who hid his master's money in the ground rather than take the risk of investing it

- **Dramatic false consolation.** It feels like dramatic consolation, and I firmly believe that it is dramatic consolation, but all the wise, loving people around me are worried about me and are disagreeing with my inspirations. I am manic and I don't know it. I want to save the world, but on my terms and with me as the savior. I am a zealous apostle, but I make sure that I am center stage rather than Christ. I am manipulative, stubborn, and close minded toward the people who love me and care for me. Everyone else is trying to slow me down, but I act with an urgency that everyone else believes is rash and unwarranted.

  ○ Biblical images:

    - The zealots who wanted to carry off Jesus to make him king
    - The scribes and Pharisees who, in the name of God, seek to destroy Jesus
    - Moses, when he kills the Egyptian for beating an Israelite

- **Placid false consolation.** I believe that I am in placid consolation, but what I'm calling "at peace" is actually lethargy. I appear to myself to be quietly doing the work of God—a placid pond. In reality I am paralyzed, inactive, absent, avoiding—a dying lake that has no oxygen and therefore cannot sustain life.

- ○ Biblical images:

    - ▪ King Solomon at the end of his life, living comfortably while his people slide into poverty, desolation, and idolatry
    - ▪ Nicodemus, who had the desire to follow Jesus but not the conviction, courage, or generosity
    - ▪ The comfortable rich man in the parable who builds more barns in which to store his abundant wealth

- **Dramatic difficult consolation.** I'm sad, angry, lonely, or depressed, but I know my God stands by me and I refuse to abandon God or my faith. I am tempted to do something dramatic, like leave my marriage or my job, but I recognize that it's the depression talking, so I'm not going to act on those feelings. I'm determined to find healthy ways to cope with and express my strong negative emotions. I rely on my good friends, family, and spiritual mentors to support me and give me advice during this difficult time.

    - ○ Biblical images:

        - ▪ Job, who is furious but never stops talking to God and listening for God and who never abandons his wife even though she has given up on him
        - ▪ The psalmist, who frequently feels distressed but continues to turn over his inner pain to God and

who trusts that God will rescue him. "How Long, O Lord . . .?" (Psalm 13)

- The woman who desperately pleads with Jesus to heal her daughter, saying, "Even the dogs eat the scraps that fall from the table"

- **Placid difficult consolation.** I'm feeling lethargic, but I force myself to get up and go to work. I make a firm commitment to stay loyal to my relationships, my work, and so on, even though I don't feel like doing anything. I would rather escape life and hide in my room today, but I know that this feeling will pass, and in the meantime I will use my firm will to act out of faith, hope, and love. I will rely on my healthy support system (my family, friends) to help me through the day.

  ○ Biblical images:

    - Qoheleth, who is a bit depressed and disillusioned but stays faithful anyway. Unlike Job, he's not furious or despairing, but like Job he continues to address God and to stay faithful to his godly life.
    - Moses, in the desert with the Israelites. He is frustrated and tired but continues to work with God and with the people he is called to lead. He takes one step at a time, not giving in to despair or letting his people do so.

Notes

_____

_____

_____

_____

_____

_____

_____

_____

_____

_____

_____

_____

_____

_____

_____

_____

_____

Notes

9

Idea #9: Our Primary Focus Should Be on Discernment of Spirits, Not Discernment of Choices

When I first set out to write *God's Voice Within*, a book about Ignatian discernment, my vision of the book was quite different from the end result. In fact, I tell friends that I actually wrote two books on discernment, but no one will ever see the first one. The working title of the first manuscript was "Nine Steps to a Good Decision." I wanted to write a book wherein a person who had a decision to make could pick up my book, follow the nine steps presented therein, and *voila!*, the answer would pop out the other end. I was mostly done with the first draft when, as novice director, I had to make a big and important decision. I decided to use, concretely, the nine steps as a trial run. It was a disaster! Why? You can probably guess: spiritual decision making simply does not proceed in such a mathematical, systematic way. The Holy Spirit is far too wild to be domesticated that way.

And so I scrapped the first manuscript and returned to reflection mode, asking myself, "How, then, does an Ignatian person come to a decision?" And I discovered the reason

Ignatius wrote more about discernment of *spirits* than about discernment of *choices*. The reason we make bad choices is because we discern the spirits badly—or to put it in a more optimistic light: if we discern the spirits well, then the decisions will flow out of us naturally.

North Americans are a product-centered people. Talk and reflection are worthless to us if the concrete and visible result does not immediately follow. Because of this we are impatient with the seemingly amorphous stages of discernment. We want the step-by-step directions that will get us to our destination with no meanderings. But because we are talking about communication with God, most of the process of good discernment is organic and somewhat vague. We need to make our peace with that fact.

So, in the end, I wrote a manuscript that I called *Ignatian Intuition*.[15] The skill we need is not logical or rational reasoning but rather a spiritual intuition that can tell us when our thoughts, dreams, and emotions are in sync with God and when they aren't. We can then gently, haltingly, ever so slowly move toward God. In the slow process of doing this discernment of spirits and moving toward the good spirit, we will come to our decision. Or better: the decision will come to us. We gradually begin to realize which way is the right way to go. We will "come to see" the answer, rather than "make a decision." It will be as though God and our soul have already made their decision and they are only now informing us of it.

Contemporary psychology backs up this idea. Renowned psychologist Ap Dijksterhuis and his collaborators have introduced the idea of unconscious thought theory, or UTT, which is

> an attempt to understand the different roles conscious and unconscious deliberation play in decision making. At a high level, this theory proposes that for decisions that require the application of strict rules, the conscious mind must be involved. For example, if you need to do a math calculation, only your conscious mind is able to follow the precise arithmetic rules needed for correctness. On the other hand, for decisions that involve large amounts of information and multiple vague, and perhaps even conflicting, constraints, your unconscious mind is well suited to tackle the issue. UTT hypothesizes that this is due to the fact that these regions of your brain have more neuronal bandwidth available, allowing them to move around more information and sift through more potential solutions than your conscious centers of thinking. Your conscious mind, according to this theory, is like a home computer on which you can run carefully written programs that return correct answers to limited problems, whereas your unconscious mind is like Google's vast data centers, in which statistical algorithms sift through terabytes of unstructured information, teasing out surprisingly useful solutions to difficult questions.[16]

It is a trap, therefore, to think that we should perfect the conscious process of making the decision. Instead, we should learn to discern the spirits well and then the decisions will flow naturally from there.

Notes

Notes

10

Idea #10: What Is Consolation without Previous Cause?

This is how Ignatius defines the experience of consolation without previous cause:

> God alone can give consolation to the soul without any previous cause. It belongs solely to the Creator to come into a soul, to leave it, to act upon it, to draw it wholly to the love of His Divine Majesty. I said without previous cause, that is, without any preceding perception or knowledge of any subject by which a soul might be led to such a consolation through its own acts of intellect and will. (Rule 2, Second Week)

Ignatian practitioners don't talk much these days about consolation without previous cause. I suspect the reason for the silence is that we don't have a clear idea of what it is. Even the experts don't seem to agree.[17]

In fact, the renowned Ignatian expert Jules Toner many years ago wrote an entire essay on the "diverse interpretations" of Ignatian scholars.[18] The various opinions fall into one of two camps. One side argues that it is an ordinary and common experience. The other side argues that if it is truly without previous cause, then it must be so rare as to be almost nonexistent. At a

conference, I once heard a Jesuit put forward this second opin-
ion. He believed that if one could name any consoling factors
leading up to the experience of consolation, then the consolation had a previous cause and therefore did not fit the criterion.
In the end, he had no examples of its occurrence, either from
his own life or from his long years of ministry in spiritual and
retreat direction. At one point he asked the audience if anyone thought they might have an example of consolation without
previous cause. I raised my hand and told the following story
from my own life:

> I have wanted to be a priest almost since before I can
> remember. But I knew only diocesan priests and so I had
> no notion of joining religious life. As a high school senior, I
> began the application process to join the regional diocesan
> seminary. All was going well. Then one day at my rural public
> high school, my buddy told me that one of our teachers said
> that I should become a Jesuit. We both had a good chuckle
> about it and moved on. That was "second period" in my high
> school day. In "third period," I was in the library working on
> notecards for a research paper when, all of a sudden, I was
> overwhelmed with the notion of becoming a Jesuit. What
> was crazy about that was that I knew practically nothing
> about them, nor did I know any of them personally. But here I
> was, in the library of a public high school, flooded with great
> desires to become one. I looked up from my notecards and
> said to my friend, "Tiffany, what the hell am I going to do with
> my life?" She laughed, scribbled something on a notecard,
> and handed it to me. It said, "Mark Thibodeaux. Diagnosis:
> Senioritis. By Doctor Tiffany Hidalgo. January 29, 1988." I took
> that notecard and folded it up and put it in my wallet. I did
> so because something told me that I would want to have a
> memento of this moment for the rest of my life.
>
> About a week later, I called the Jesuits in Grand
> Coteau—only eleven miles from my house—and asked,
> "Could I speak to a Jesuit?" I drove there a few days later

and spoke to the one who happened to answer the phone. I remember starting the conversation with, "So, what's a Jesuit?" A few weeks later, I began the application process. A few months later, I entered the novitiate. Decades later, as a happy Jesuit priest, I have that notecard framed in my office. It's one of my most prized possessions.

At the end of my story, the Jesuit presenter said, "Well, that's a nice story, but the teacher saying that you should be a Jesuit is the previous cause, so that is not an example of consolation without previous cause."

Long after Ignatius's time, psychology and philosophy have taught us that it is impossible to have any human experience purely "without cause." This side of heaven, there is no such thing as an entirely unmediated experience. Every human experience is inextricably connected to our past, our biology and psychology, and so on. Therefore, if we insist on the strictest interpretation of the concept of consolation without previous cause—if we insist that it must be *purely* without cause—then we must discard the concept altogether as the mistaken result of an outdated understanding of human nature. Indeed, some Ignatian scholars have come to see this whole concept as obsolete or unhelpful.[19]

But I think we would be wrong to dismiss the insight of St. Ignatius. He had his finger on the pulse of some unusual experience that he observed in himself and others. He was trying to put a name to that experience and was severely limited by a lack of vocabulary and by his 16th-century understanding. But if the spiritual experience was real, then it probably happens to us as well. And if Ignatius felt he needed a name for the experience, then we probably need a name for it too.

So, let me show my hand and take a stab at the experience to which Ignatius was referring. I propose that consolation without previous cause is the spiritual experience wherein the *intensity* of consolation we experience is far out of proportion to the preceding cause.[20] In the example above, my teacher's innocuous comment should not have caused such a joyous inner response and the subsequent set of behaviors that changed the trajectory of my life. It was only a small, passing remark—not even made in my presence, for heaven's sake! I have told my story of the notecard many times over the years, and often people excitedly respond by sharing a similar story from their own lives—moments when the entire trajectory of their lives shifted in a moment of joy and serendipity. Clearly, this is an experience wholly different from typical consolation. And because it is such an important experience, we need a name for it. We need some way to articulate this human experience and distinguish it from ordinary spiritual experiences. I believe that this is what Ignatius was getting at when introducing what he called consolation without previous cause.

Needless to say, this type of experience is rare. In my own life, I can point to no other experience like my "notecard moment." We should conclude that consolation without previous cause is an extremely rare, perhaps once-in-a-lifetime experience, right?

Well, yes and no.

Earlier, when speaking of "regular" consolation, I proposed that it might be helpful to distinguish between dramatic consolation and placid consolation. I also suggested that we could make this dramatic-placid distinction regarding all the states of being. Here I would propose that, as in the other states, one could experience dramatic consolation without previous cause or placid consolation without previous cause. My vocation story is obviously an example of the dramatic type. Here is an example of a placid consolation without previous cause:

> Several years ago while living in Cambridge, Massachusetts, I had an experience of placid consolation without previous cause. I woke up on a very ordinary day with nothing special on my calendar or on my mind. I like to meditate first thing in the morning, so after a strong cup of coffee and doing a few other trivial things, I headed toward prayer. This is a daily routine for me. However, on this particular morning, I felt the Lord's presence urging me to get to my prayer chair *now*. It felt as though the Lord was so looking forward to being with me that he impatiently prodded me to meet him there. I felt myself smiling and saying, "I'm coming, I'm coming, Lord" throughout my morning routine. Just before moving to my prayer chair, I started to put on a pair of warm socks (as a Cajun in Massachusetts in the winter, this is not optional!). Between my first and second sock, I was "taken" by God. I felt an overwhelming peace and presence fill my whole being. I just sat there in a trance on the edge of my bed, with one foot socked and the other bare. After a moment or two, I recovered enough to put on the second sock and move to my prayer chair. My prayer was filled with a deep sense of God's loving presence. When the prayer ended, I stood up and got moving into my ordinary day. Here's the kicker: unlike in my notecard story, nothing really changed about my life because of that experience. There was no remarkable "content" to the prayer time; no decision was made; no miraculous healing or life-changing epiphany occurred. The rest of my day was as ordinary as the day before. And yet, here I am, more than fifteen years later, recounting the story, and I can remember the experience as though it happened yesterday.

I once heard a Jesuit call this type of experience "the Big Kiss." Sometimes it seems that God just wants to give us a Big Kiss. God is not trying to change the trajectory of our lives or reveal a divine secret. God just wants to give us a Big Kiss for no particular reason other than that God loves us irresistibly. Unlike the notecard story, I've had numerous such experiences as the sock moment—times when I felt that I was more joyful than I had a right to be, more hopeful than the moment called for, more at peace than this world could ever promise. From time to time, God seems to give me a random, inexplicable, uncalled-for Big Kiss. Note that I am not claiming that my sock moment had no cause; I probably could name a few reasons I might have felt consoled and joyful on that cold Massachusetts morning, but the spontaneous, punch-drunk joy that I felt in the moment between socks was far out of proportion to any of my ordinary reasons to be happy that day.

As with my notecard story, I've told this story many times, and people often can't wait for me to finish so that they can tell their version of the sock moment. Every devout Christian seems to have an occasional inexplicable moment of consolation that seems out of proportion to any of the "causes" that might have precipitated it.

We need a name for this experience, and Ignatius provides us with one: *consolation without previous cause.*

Notes

_____

_____

_____

_____

_____

_____

_____

_____

_____

_____

_____

_____

_____

_____

_____

_____

_____

_____

Notes

11

Idea #11: Beware of the Moments Just after Consolation without Previous Cause

Ignatius cautions us about the time immediately following consolation without previous cause:

> When consolation is without previous cause, as was said, there can be no deception in it, since it can proceed from God our Lord only. But a spiritual person who has received such a consolation must consider it very attentively, and must cautiously distinguish the actual time of the consolation from the period which follows it. At such a time the soul is still fervent and favored with the grace and aftereffects of the consolation which has passed. In this second period the soul frequently forms various resolutions and plans which are not granted directly by God our Lord. They may come from our own reasoning on the relations of our concepts and on the consequences of our judgments, or they may come from the good or evil spirit. Hence, they must be carefully examined before they are given full approval and put into execution. (Rule Eight, Second Week)

If it is correct to say that the experience of consolation without previous cause is indeed a regular, if not frequent, occurrence, then Ignatius's warning is crucial. I have found both in my own spiritual life and in directing others that the time immediately following such an experience is a tricky time when the false spirit will try to get the better of us. It is for this reason that Ignatius warns us not to make a "hasty vow" when we are feeling great fervor: "If the one who is giving the Exercises sees that the exercitant is going on in consolation and in great fervor, he must admonish him not to be inconsiderate or hasty in making any promise or vow."[21]

Anyone who works in youth retreat ministry knows about the dangers of the "retreat high." If a youth retreat goes well and the retreatants are deeply moved by the end of it, they often feel an extraordinary happiness that makes them a little giddy. Often, this will lead to imprudent and irrational behavior such as immediately breaking up with a girlfriend or boyfriend or vowing to pray daily for an unreasonable quantity of time. This phenomenon is so common that leaders sometimes warn retreatants about it near the end of the retreat. And while it is easier to observe in youth because of their inclinations toward high drama, the retreat-high experience is almost as prevalent in adults.

Here are two other examples.

First example: I once directed a novice, Justin, whose eight-day Spiritual Exercises retreat was unusually consoling. He was a self-proclaimed "high-energy/hyperactive" kind of guy, and the primary grace of the retreat was that of the Lord training him to gently quiet his soul and experience God in stillness for long stretches of time. However, early into Day Eight he had an experience of the resurrected Lord that left him feeling extraordinarily happy. He felt as though he had just had the best prayer experience of his lifetime. However, the hours following that prayer time were torturous for him. He was "too excited" and could not keep still. He struggled with the silence for the first time on the retreat and was unable to calm himself enough to enter back into contemplative prayer. He was confused by the strange fact that his best prayer time would actually leave him unable to pray again. When he told me all of this in direction that day, I read to him Ignatius's warning about "the period that follows" an extraordinary spiritual experience. Together we strategized about how to fortify himself against the false spirit and how to get back to prayer in whatever way he could (for him, that meant taking a very long walk and praying the rosary, calmly asking Mary to take him back to her Son). This strategy worked well, and he was able to finish the retreat in peace again.

Second example: A friend of mine who is a parish priest once told me that he sometimes experiences a "high" after a wonderfully consoling string of Sunday-morning Masses wherein the liturgies are prayerful and uplifting and the congregation exits with joy and peace in their hearts. He told me that an older parish priest once cautioned him about Sunday afternoons, saying that coming down off the high of the Sunday-morning Masses can be disorienting and emotionally challenging. My friend told me that he has to be attentive and intentional about how he spends his Sunday afternoons, lest he behave poorly as he descends from the emotional heights.

From a psychological perspective, what might be going on here? Why would someone be particularly susceptible to the false spirit just after consolation without previous cause? A therapist I know once said a funny thing: "The problem with being vulnerable is that . . . you're vulnerable!"[22] By that he meant that at the very moment that one is appropriately vulnerable (to God or to one's spouse, for example) that person is also vulnerable to other people or experiences as well. Putting it in Ignatian vocabulary, we could say it this way—The extraordinary vulnerability one experiences in consolation without previous cause leaves one extraordinarily vulnerable to *both* spirits—the good one and the false one. During the prayerful experience itself, the person is safe in the protection of the divine moment, but the false spirit could attempt to pounce on the lingering vulnerability just after the consolation.

Notes

_____

_____

_____

_____

_____

_____

_____

_____

_____

_____

_____

_____

_____

_____

_____

_____

_____

_____

_____

Notes

12

Idea #12: Ignatius's Insight about Being Cautious in the Time Immediately after Consolation without Previous Cause Also Must Be Applied to Ignatius's "First Time" of Making a Decision.

In another section of the Spiritual Exercises commonly known as the "Rules for Election," Ignatius gives us "three times when we might make an election." He says the first time is when "God our Lord so moves and attracts the will that a devout soul without hesitation, or the possibility of hesitation, follows what has been manifested to it."[23] Ignatius never equates this "first time" with the experience of consolation without previous cause, but it seems obvious that he is speaking about the same thing, or at least that they are closely related. It seems to me, therefore, that we should carefully apply the rules for consolation without previous cause as we begin to take action in this First Time.

Applying those rules, we would find ourselves healthily "doubting" the discernment after all. We would test the decision to verify that we are not being swept away by the wiles of the false spirit. While Ignatius says that we aren't able to doubt the decision in this First Time, he warns those who have experienced consolation without previous cause that the experience *immediately after* the consolation could very well come from the false spirit. An experience of consolation without previous cause could almost immediately turn into a moment of false consolation wherein a feeling of mania will lead us to make rash decisions.

The bottom line is that, even though I am "without being able to doubt" the experience, I should indeed test the spirits to make sure that I'm not operating under a false consolation that sometimes immediately follows consolation without previous cause.[24]

Take my notecard story above. I believe that this experience was a dramatic consolation without previous cause, and I also believe it was an experience wherein I was not able to doubt. I remember well that my strange desire to be a Jesuit was simply overwhelming and that it seemed to have come from some otherworldly place. I had an exuberance that I could not explain. I was almost shaking with excitement. And remember: I knew not a single Jesuit and hardly knew anything about them! When I read St. Ignatius's description of that first time when a decision is made, I am confident that this is what I experienced that day. Without having the vocabulary to describe it back then, I was certainly without being able to doubt God's wildly consoling presence in the experience.

So, interiorly, I was without being able to doubt. But exteriorly, every wise person I consulted (and I, myself) did indeed test the experience for its authenticity. After having this inexplicable joy for a day or two, I went to see my diocesan parish priest, an incredibly wise and savvy spiritual director named Michael Guidry. I told him my story (he knew me very well by then and was accompanying me through the application process with the diocese). After hearing the whole thing, he said, "Okay, this is what I think you should do. Give the Jesuits a call, tell them your story, and see what happens. The Jesuits don't tend to take people at your age, so if they don't send you away, then perhaps it is a sign from God."

And, of course, the Society itself did not say, "Clearly this is a case of 'without being able to doubt,' so let's advance him to First Vows right away." I went through the thorough application process and did months of direction before entering. Of course, I did two years of novitiate, testing the call before being admitted to First Vows, which in turn only advanced me to the next stages of the "long and exacting tests" that Ignatius prescribes for Jesuits in formation.[25]

My parish priest, the Society, and even I intuited what Ignatius wrote about when describing the moments after consolation without previous cause. There are times when the euphoric feelings of that dramatic consolation could lead us to be deceived and to make what Ignatius would call a "hasty vow."[26]

Notes

Notes

_____

_____

_____

_____

_____

_____

_____

_____

_____

_____

_____

_____

_____

_____

_____

_____

PART TWO

EMPLOYING DISCERNMENT OF SPIRITS
AS A SPIRITUAL DIRECTOR
OR PASTORAL COUNSELOR

The most important question I ask myself when I am working with someone in spiritual direction or pastoral counseling is this: "What state of being is this person in? In desolation, consolation, false consolation, or difficult consolation?"[27] I avoid making any bold moves until I have at least a good guess as to the answer to this question. Why? Because Ignatius rightly tells me that a director should treat the directee differently depending on the spiritual state she is in.[28]

How so? How does a director treat a directee differently in the various spiritual states?

13

Accompanying Someone through Desolation

There are eight important things that I try to keep in mind when I am working with a directee who is in desolation.

I encourage greater dependency on her support network.
Ignatius says that a person in desolation has the false spirit as her counselor.[29] Therefore she will not be able to rely on her own instincts and judgment at that moment. Instead, she should hand over the car keys—so to speak—of her decisions to the people around her who have good judgment and who care for her: her spiritual advisers, her family, her healthy friends. She should also lean on the support services of her church, such as the sacraments, communal prayer experiences, and the wisdom and teaching of the church.

If I am her spiritual director or counselor, it might be good to see her at a greater frequency than normal until she has passed through this difficult time. I may also have to be more assertive with her. Again, she is driving under the influence of the false spirit, so I may need to take the car keys from her—and she may not give them up easily. For example, a person in desolation may be more inclined to keep secrets from her director.[30] I may have to ask her a lot of direct and perhaps even embarrassing questions and will have to press her until she gives me the whole story. I may also have to give more direct and concrete instructions regarding how to act, how to pray, what *not* to do, and so on. It is true that spiritual directors are not, generally, supposed to give advice and lead directees to specific conclusions or actions. However, periods of desolation sometimes require a firmer hand.

Together, we name and normalize it.

Sometimes, it is better *not* to name it desolation—particularly for a beginner or immature directee—because it might frighten her and make it worse. But often, I as a director can console the directee by pointing out to her that this is desolation and that this experience is a common one in the spiritual life. One example of the dramatic, sweeping negative conclusion that is characteristic of desolation is a belief that one's experience is all the more terrible because it is an aberration and is not a part of a "holy" person's spiritual life. Exposing and dispelling that lie may help tremendously. I once had a novice describing at length his upsetting state of mind and heart. After he finished, I said to him, "You know, this is a textbook example of Ignatius's understanding of desolation." I then pointed out to him how the things he described were all laid out in the Rules for Discernment of Spirits. A broad smile suddenly appeared on his face and he said, "Wow, you're right! Well, if this is just plain old desolation, then I can handle that!" And indeed he did.

Together, we seek understanding.

A psychologist I know once defined the term *trauma* as "experience seeking articulation." She said that when a person has an experience she has no way of articulating for herself, it is traumatic for her. For example, if I call you "friend" and then you betray me, it is traumatic to me because the experience (the betrayal) does not fit the label that I've given it ("friendship"). Once I find a way to articulate the experience ("a friend made a mistake"), then it'll still hurt, but it won't be so traumatic anymore.

The same is true for desolation. It is a traumatic experience because the person has not yet found a way to articulate the experience. Once she has put into words what she is experiencing, she may still be in desolation, but it won't be nearly as traumatic. And sometimes, finding the proper articulation can quickly lead to a way out of the desolation.

And so, as a director, I work with the person to help her find words to describe what she's experiencing. Ignatius says that "we must carefully observe the whole course of our thoughts . . . the beginning and middle and end."[31] So I will ask my directee lots of questions: "When did you begin to feel this way? What do you think brought it on? What does it feel like? Are there circumstantial factors that are leading you to feel bad (you're burned out, sleep deprived)? Are you unconsciously upset about something (often we might be hiding from ourselves an uncomfortable truth)?"

We could also explore helpful descriptors for the desolation: Is it emotional desolation? Spiritual? Psychological? Is it dramatic desolation or placid desolation?

Note that, at this moment, we are not trying to fix the problem. Because the false spirit is the directee's counselor, it is *not* a good time to make big changes in one's life. This sort of thing is best done when the directee is in consolation and is listening to the counsel of the good spirit. Our objective here is to observe, understand, and articulate the experience well. Doing so will alleviate the trauma of the experience and will dispose the directee to the grace of healing and of moving toward consolation.

Together, we expose the lies and twisted truths.

St. Ignatius says that in desolation the false spirit brings "fallacious reasonings, subtleties, and continual deceptions."[32] This is well said. Sometimes a desolate person is acting on downright lies ("persistent fallacies") and other times they aren't so much lies as twisted truths ("subtleties"). Either way, as a director I can help the person by getting her to state clearly, explicitly, and succinctly what lies and twisted truths are being whispered in her ear at the moment. I like to ask it bluntly: "What do you think the false spirit is telling you right now? How is that a fallacy or a twisted truth? What might you think the good spirit is telling you right now?" (Often, the directee can't hear the voice of the good spirit during desolation, but with the director she can speculate what the good spirit *would* be telling her, *were* she able to hear it.) Sometimes I encourage the person to write out all the lies and twisted truths. That way, when she hears them whispered in her thoughts, she will recognize them straightaway and can resist being carried away by them. She might also write out the statements that we both agree are probably messages from the good spirit. She can read these statements to herself regularly for encouragement and to regain a sense of balance when the false spirit is wreaking havoc.

There are two rather common categories of lies or twisted truths that I'll want to look out for. First, people in desolation tend to make *sweeping and dramatic judgments* about God, themselves, other people, and about what is going on in their lives. For example, my friend fails to say hello to me when I pass her in the hallway, and I conclude, "She never really liked me."

Here is another more dramatic and embarrassing example from my own life: Once, when I had several days of desolation on my annual retreat, I went into the director's office and said, "I don't think I know how to pray at all. I think I've been faking it all these years." This was when I had been a Jesuit for years and had already published a book on prayer!

Second, a desolate person is often *afraid of some future catastrophe* that is all the scarier because it is vague and not yet articulated. As a director, I like to ask, "What's the worst-case scenario here? What's the worst thing that could happen?" A lot of times, the person will describe a future that is either not at all likely or not nearly as frightening as it felt before she articulated it. Once, as a high school teacher, I worked with a boy who was honest, smart, and even holy but who got caught cheating. He was confused as to why he allowed himself to do this. After a while, he was able to say that there was some vague fear in him at the moment he chose to cheat. I asked, "What was the fear?" At first, he honestly couldn't say. But after teasing out some of his thoughts and feelings, he found himself saying, "I was afraid of failing the test." I knew how smart this kid was, so I asked, "How many times have you actually failed a test in your whole life?" He answered, "Never." The false spirit had convinced him of a lie but kept the details of the lie buried in his subconscious. The result was a vague and frightening dread. If he had been able to name the lie at the moment he was taking the test, he would not have been taken in by it.

I encourage a moratorium on unnecessary decisions.

Everyone is familiar with Ignatius's Fifth Rule of the First Set: A person in desolation should avoid making any decisions since she is not in a right mind to do so. Why is this such a critical rule? Because a desolate person is extremely uncomfortable and will be tempted to do anything to get herself to a more comfortable place. Psychologically speaking, a person feels empowered when she makes a firm decision. This empowerment takes away some of the sting of powerlessness that a desolate person feels. So, then, this is how the whole thing shakes down: First, the desolate person feels powerless, and then she unwittingly makes a bad decision. Having "taken control" of her life by making a (bad) decision, she now feels empowered. Finally, she interprets this feeling of empowerment as a "confirmation" of her (bad) decision, and this brings her even more happiness. Backing up and looking at this entire process, we see that this person has moved from desolation to false consolation, as is described in the previous section.[33]

I am gentle and encouraging toward the directee.

Ignatius has some beautiful things to say about the gentleness with which we should treat a person in desolation:

> When one is in desolation, he should be mindful that God has left him to his natural powers to resist the different agitations and temptations of the enemy in order to try him. He can resist with the help of God, which always remains, though he may not clearly perceive it. For though God has taken from him the abundance of fervor and overflowing love and the intensity of His favors, nevertheless, he has sufficient grace for eternal salvation.[34]

> If the director of the Exercises observes that the exercitant is in desolation and tempted, let him not deal severely and harshly with him, but gently and kindly. He should encourage and strengthen him for the future by exposing to him the wiles of the enemy of our human nature, and by getting him to prepare and dispose himself for the coming consolation.[35]

It is clear, then, that my role as director of a desolate person is that of encourager, uplifter, and consoler.[36] I should find ways to make the person feel a little better, to remind her that this experience is only temporary and that God's love is present even when she doesn't feel it. How might I console my directee?

I draw hope and optimism out of her. Most people try to make others feel better by naming things about the other that they find encouraging, hopeful, and good. But a more effective way to make a person feel better is to *get her to name such things herself.* It's entirely possible—maybe even likely—that the things in her life that make you feel better are not the same things that make her feel better. So, then, I don't say, "You should feel better because you've got ___ and ___ and ___ in your life." Instead, I try to tease out her own encouragements that she simply hasn't said out loud lately. So, I ask: "What keeps you going? What sustains you in this difficult time? What gives you strength and hope? What are you grateful for? What good desires are you experiencing right now? What happy memories bring you comfort?"

I remind her that this experience is only temporary. One characteristic of desolation is that the person subconsciously believes that this miserable feeling will last forever. I can help her remember, then, that desolation comes and goes, and that soon enough she'll be in consolation again. If I've been working with her for a while, I might be able to say, "Remember last year when you had that tough month or so? You felt like it would last forever, but it didn't, did it? In the same way, this too shall pass. You just need to hold on for now."

I might even use Ignatius's own words. People with Ignatian training remember that Ignatius famously said, "When in consolation, prepare for desolation," but we mysteriously forget that he also said the opposite: that the directee in desolation "prepare and dispose himself for the coming consolation."[37] These words could be deeply comforting to someone in the dark valley of desolation. "I know you're in a painful place right now," I could say, "but Ignatius is telling you that consolation is on the way and you need to prepare yourself for it!"

I remind her that God's love is present even when she doesn't feel it. Again, the words of Ignatius might make the point all the stronger. God's divine help, he says, "always remains, though [the person] may not clearly perceive it."[38] For reasons that are mysterious to us, God seems distant at times. It's a painful reality to accept, and yet comforting to know that it is a common human experience and that even the doctors and mystics of the church were not exempt. The Three "Teresas" (Lisieux, Ávila, and Calcutta), for example, all experienced painful spiritual seasons wherein they struggled to hear God's voice or feel God's presence. It's corny, but you could ask the retreatant if she still believes in the sun at midnight or in the love of her friends even when they are far away.

I am firm with the false spirit.

Although we are to be gentle and kind to the directee, we should be firm and stern in the face of the false spirit. Here is how Ignatius puts it:

> Though in desolation we must never change our former resolutions, it will be very advantageous to intensify our activity against the desolation. We can insist more upon prayer, upon meditation, and on much examination of ourselves. We can make an effort in a suitable way to do some penance.[39]

Being gentle and indulgent with the directee does *not* mean allowing the directee to be gentle and indulgent with the false spirit. This is an important point, because her desolation could easily lead her to become lethargic or slothful in regard to her spiritual life. This, of course, will only make things worse. While being easy on herself in other aspects of her life (allowing herself a little more relaxation time), she must resolve herself to work ever harder on her spiritual life, keeping firm in her commitments to prayer, the church, and so on.

As her director, I too must do battle with the false spirit. Ignatius is not ambiguous here: we are to "change ourselves intensely against the false spirit." I must assertively—perhaps even aggressively—expose and dispel the lies, twisted truths, pessimistic attitudes, and unhealthy behaviors of my directee.

Jesuit spiritual writer David Fleming has a perfect contemporary metaphor to explain Ignatius's Twelfth Rule of the First Week:

> The evil spirit often behaves like a spoiled child. If a person is firm with children, children give up petulant ways of acting. But if a person shows indulgence or weakness in any way, children are merciless in trying to get what they want, stomping their feet in defiance or wheedling their way into favor. So our tactics must include firmness in dealing with the evil spirit in our lives.[40]

One way in which I will need to be firm is by not allowing despair to creep in. The therapist Steven Levenkron says that at times he needs to be "warm and bossy" with his clients.[41] So, I will not tolerate brooding, wallowing, or self-castigating. "We have too much work to do!" I'll say, reminding my directee that Ignatius says that she "can do much" in desolation.[42] How can I encourage her to "do much"? I often ask the directee to name for me the things she does that give her life, such as exercising and spending time with loved ones. I then ask her to name aloud things that she does that are life sapping, such as isolating herself or drinking too much.[43] I ask her to make two lists: one list for her life-affirming activities and the other for her life-sapping ones. I ask her to commit to doing the things on her life-affirming list and to avoid doing the things on the life-sapping list.

So, putting it all together, we see that as a director I must be gentle and kind with the directee (warm) while at the same time doing battle with the false spirit dwelling within her (bossy). The directee herself will make it more difficult because she will be inclined to do the opposite: to do battle with herself (to punish herself for "allowing this to happen") and to be gentle and indulgent with the false spirit (entertaining its discouraging and pessimistic thoughts). Now we see well the delicate and tricky work of the director! This work will not be easy. I will have to do a lot of on-the-spot discernment to determine when to push and when to pat. I like to imagine that the directee has a stubborn little gremlin inside her that I must grab by the scruff and muzzle, all the while giving kind words and assurances to the "patient."

I am cautious about my own proclivity to desolation.

A wise saying has been passed down from one Jesuit novice director to the next: "When a novice enters your office with a monkey on his back, do what you can to help him get it off of him. But make sure that monkey doesn't jump on your back." Desolation is contagious. I can catch it from my directee if I am not diligent about my own spiritual and psychological well-being. When working with someone in desolation, I need to do my own work to make sure that I'm leaving it behind me as I leave my office at the end of the day. I need my own pressure-release valves that allow me to process the experience and to let it go.

Notes

Notes

_____

_____

_____

_____

_____

_____

_____

_____

_____

_____

_____

_____

_____

_____

_____

_____

14

Accompanying Someone through Difficult Consolation

As explained earlier, what I call difficult consolation is the experience of having desolate feelings (sadness, anger, spiritual aridity) while in fact remaining in consolation—that is, while remaining in sync with God and still desiring to be faithful, hopeful, and loving. Part of why I feel we need a name for this state of being is because it is so common in the spiritual life. As a director or pastoral minister, I frequently work with people who are in difficult consolation. How should I minister to them?

There are four important things to keep in mind when I am working with a directee who is in difficult consolation.

I give a lot of affirmation and encouragement.

While not denying the bad news of the feelings of desolation, I proclaim the good news that the directee is in fact in consolation. I show her the ways in which it is clear to me that, despite her feelings, she remains on God's path. And I show her the ways in which her great desires to be faithful, hopeful, and loving stand out to me. I draw self-affirmation out of her by asking, "What is it that continues to sustain you and give you hope through the tough days?" I might say, "You know, it's clear to me that this is a difficult moment, but it's also clear to me that you are 'keeping the faith' through it all. How is it that you have done so?"

I help her to fortify her defenses.

One of my novices, Vincent Moore, recently described his experience of difficult consolation as keeping spiritually steady despite continuously "being invited" to desolation by the false spirit. This is a good description of difficult consolation: a moment in my life when I am acutely being tempted to give in to the "invitations" of the false spirit. Therefore, as director I work with the person in building up good defenses against such invitations. How so?

First, I help her to articulate the ways in which she is invited to desolation. "What exactly is the voice in your head inviting you to do, think, or feel? What desolate thoughts are you tempted to run with? What desolate feelings are you tempted to be swept away by?" Naming the temptations will help her look out for and resist them.

Second, we work together to name the "holes in the fortress walls"—the vulnerabilities wherein the false spirit can invade the castle.[44] For example, when stressed or feeling down, is she prone to anger? To fear? To judgmentalism? We then brainstorm about how she might fortify herself in those vulnerable areas of her spirit and personality.

**I encourage her to be gentle on herself and
hard on the false spirit.**

As in desolation, a common temptation is to do the opposite:
to be overly self-critical and to entertain negative thoughts and
judgments proposed by the false spirit.

I encourage her to hold off on any decisions.

Difficult consolation is the only type of true consolation
wherein it is better to avoid making changes or important decisions. Because she is experiencing "invitations" from the false
spirit, she will be susceptible to making poor decisions. My
own novice master used to say, "When you're riding on a horse
through the desert and a bad sandstorm kicks up, get off your
horse, put your face to the ground, and just wait for it to pass."

Notes

Notes

_____

_____

_____

_____

_____

_____

_____

_____

_____

_____

_____

_____

_____

_____

_____

_____

_____

15

Accompanying Someone through False Consolation

Let us recall what false consolation is: a spiritual state of being wherein the person experiences feelings of consolation and therefore is convinced that she is in consolation, when in fact she has turned down a wrong path into a blind alley. Although the direction she is going in looks good and feels good on the surface, the directee is in fact moving away from God and from God's will for her. To put it another way, the directee is attracted to good things that she is not in fact called to by God. To give a couple of examples:

- Lupe has become obsessed with her volunteer work at the homeless shelter while her marriage and family are in crisis.
- Arjun is attracted to huge prayer commitments, fasts, and penances and doesn't realize that he is in danger of spiritual burnout.

Presuming I have correctly recognized that my directee is in false consolation, how might I help her? Directing such a person is the most delicate work of all. People in false consolation are living in a pleasurable fantasy and will resist any movement out of that fantasy. If you are not careful, the directee will either abandon your help or directly oppose you. Unfortunately, Ignatius does not give any specific advice about how to work with such a person. Therefore, you will have to do a lot of discernment of your own strategies as you walk on those eggshells.

Either pop the balloon or tether it.

A person in false consolation is floating in a fantasy balloon. Without your help, she may well float away from God and God's will and toward poor decisions. Therefore, your job as a director is to prevent the balloon from floating away. Sometimes, it's good simply to pop the balloon—shatter the fantasy—and be done with it. Other times, you'll need to act more gingerly and cleverly. You'll need to tether the balloon.

- **Pop the balloon.** By this I mean that you simply expose the falsity of this state of being. You say, "You know, I know that you're feeling really good about this shift in your prayer and thinking, but I have to say that I'm not convinced that this is from the good spirit. I'm not convinced that this is the correct direction for you to go in." You would then point out the reasons you think the person is in false consolation. If the directee is familiar with Ignatian discernment, you could even say, "I fear you might be experiencing false consolation right now."

  Popping the balloon is the preferable course of action because it gets rid of the lies and twisted truths that have intoxicated the directee. It expels the demon so that the directee can pick herself up, turn around, and get moving in the right direction again.

- **Tether the balloon.** There is, however, a great risk involved in the assertive strategy of popping the balloon. As already mentioned, no one likes to have one's illusions shattered. Exposing the fantasy, then, might lead to one of three reactions in the directee. She might simply drift away from you, missing the next few appointments with you or ignoring your counsel. Second, she might turn on you and become argumentative or even combative. Third, she might accept your counsel but become so ashamed that she'll begin to self-loathe and overreact against the false spirit. In the example of Lupe, she might quit the shelter altogether, leaving it shorthanded and depriving herself of engaging in this life-affirming activity.

There are, then, good reasons to adopt a gentler strategy—to *contain* the fantasy and keep it from leading to harmful behavior rather than to eliminate it altogether. How might you do this? Let's again use the case of Lupe as our example.

First, you could try to *shift focus* a bit. First, allow her to speak at length about her work at the shelter and affirm her in this work. But then, shift the conversation to her family: "Last month, Lupe, you told me about how your daughter is really struggling right now and how your husband seems to be checked out of family life. What's the latest on this? How is your daughter now? What might you be called to do for her? How is your marriage? What might be some steps you could take toward confronting the problems in it?"

Second, you could try to *slow her down*. You could say, "Lupe, I'm delighted that your work at the shelter is going so well. I think you should keep up this great part of your life.

However, you might want to limit the hours that you work there while your family is going through this difficult time. What might be a good limit to set for yourself so that you can be fully present to the needs of your daughter?"

Third, you could get her to *reflect on how the false spirit might use this moment.* I have a Jesuit friend who frequently annoyed me by responding to some great report I was giving about my life by saying, "That's wonderful, Mark. Now, how might the false spirit use this experience?" I hated this question. I just wanted to bask in the warmth of the consoling feelings. But my older and wiser friend taught me that both spirits can use any situation to move me toward their agendas. My friend was moving me to "remain sober and alert" (see 1 Peter 5:8). And so, I might say to Lupe, "Wow! Clearly God is in this great work that you're doing. This is a victory for heaven. But, just to remain 'sober and alert' to the false spirit, Lupe, tell me, how might the false spirit use your passion and zeal to throw you off course?" No doubt, this would be an uncomfortable question—as it was when my friend first asked it of me. However, if you are in long-term direction, your directee will grow accustomed to exploring this uncomfortable though enlightening question when she is on a "high."

Treat false consolation for what it really is: desolation.

Although it should be obvious, we often forget this simple truth: false consolation is desolation. Therefore, just about all that was said earlier about how to treat desolation could be said here as well. Specifically, as a director, I should do the following for my directee:

- **Encourage her not to make any changes.** This might be even more difficult in false consolation than in desolation because the "mania" of false consolation will try to jolt the person into action. As the director, you must be the guardian of her previously well-made decisions.

- **Encourage her to rely more heavily on her support network.** Again, the mania of false consolation will give her overconfidence in her own judgment. And as in desolation, the person in false consolation will be tempted to keep secrets from her loved ones and others in her support system.

- **Be gentle on the person but firm with the false spirit.** Even if you choose to "tether the balloon" and allow the false consolation to wear itself out instead of directly confronting it, you should not tolerate misbehavior or twisted truths. You must be loving to the person but firm with the little gremlin inside the directee.

- **Steer the focus from the self to Christ.** Though on the surface the directee in false consolation will appear selfless, you as a director will be able to detect a hidden self-centeredness. As best you can, get her to look again at Christ and his actions and words in the Gospels. Make sure that her meditations are not simply musings with the self but rather actual dialogues with God.

Notes

Notes

16

Accompanying Someone through Consolation

I stay out of the way!

Ignatius tells us that "in consolation the good spirit guides and counsels us."[45] Therefore, a consoled person led by the good spirit can trust her instincts and does not need as much hand-holding as a person in desolation or one of the other states. A challenge for me as a director, then, might be to stay out of the way and let God direct the person directly. This might be particularly challenging if I have a great affection for my directee and feel joyful about her consolation. Ignatius says that the directee coming to graces and great understanding *by her own means* "produces greater spiritual relish and fruit than if [the director] had explained and developed the meaning at great length." He tells a retreat director, then, to "add only a short or summary explanation."[46]

With that said, there are a few things that a director could do with the directee.

I encourage the directee to relish this state in joy and gratitude.

After encountering the risen Christ on the road to Emmaus, the disciples exclaimed, "Were not our hearts burning within us while he spoke to us on the way?" (Luke 24:32). And the tenth leper was double blessed by Jesus when "realizing he had been healed, returned, glorifying God in a loud voice" (Luke 17:15). So, too, our directee, recognizing that she is in consolation, should return to the place where she encountered Jesus and give thanks. The directee should look back on her consoling experience and marvel, "Was not my heart burning within me?" In the spiritual life we have a wonderful word for this: *relish*. When in consolation, we relish those graces that come from it. We soak in them as in a warm bath. We suck fully from the fruits of them. Doing so will deepen and enrich the experience all the more.

As a director, I will encourage my directee to relish by asking her to tell the whole story all over again: "Wow, that's wonderful. Tell me again how it all happened. Don't leave out a single detail." As the directee rehashes the whole thing, she will receive another helping of awe, joy, and gratitude.

I will also suggest that she spend significant time "returning, glorifying God in a loud voice" by doing repetitions of the prayer passages and themes that led to the consolation, by journaling at length about the experience, by sharing the experience with loved ones, by finding concrete ways to give God thanks—through lighting a candle at church, for example, or through performing some act of charity for someone.

I encourage discernment of choices.

If it is true that "in a time of desolation we should never make any change," then it follows that consolation is the appropriate time to make a change.[47] For "in consolation the good spirit guides and counsels us."[48] Therefore, it is an ideal time to make tough decisions about one's future.

As the director, you could say, "You know, since you are in such a good space right now, why don't we revisit your question about whether or not to quit your job and pursue your dream career—the question that you wisely set aside while you were in desolation." If the directee had considered such a question in desolation, she might have been inclined to act boldly merely as a way of empowering herself in a time when she felt powerless. But, here in the state of consolation, she will be feeling content with her current life. She will more easily get to a place of Ignatian indifference about whether to quit her job. On the foundation of this indifference, she can healthily explore her options.

I encourage the directee to "prepare for desolation."

Ignatius famously instructs the one in consolation to "let him consider how he will conduct himself during the time of ensuing desolation, and store up a supply of strength as defense against that day."[49] Is Ignatius being morbid here? No, he simply is being pragmatic. It is in a time of consolation, when the good spirit is guiding us, that we can work on the spiritual and psychological issues that keep us from coping with desolation well.

Interestingly, the directee is often uninterested in doing this spiritual work and would prefer just to "relish" a bit more. Back when I was a pastoral counselor to high school boys, I noticed a common pattern among them. When they were in big trouble with their parents or with the school, they were ready to spend loads of time with me so that I could help them put out the fires they had set. But once the fire was put out, they never darkened my door again—at least until the next fire! When the crisis was resolved, I would want to meet with them some more to talk about what we might learn from this experience and long-term changes in attitude or behavior that might be needed to avert the next fire. But they were nowhere to be found. This avoidance of spiritual work is typical for an adolescent, but shouldn't we adults be willing to do this kind of work when we find that we have left desolation and entered consolation? Sadly, like adolescents, we would prefer to let the sleeping dogs of desolation lie and lazily bask in our newfound consolation.

St. Ignatius would have none of this. He would agree, I'm sure, with St. Benedict, who said, "Run while you have the light." If the directee is in consolation, then it's time for her to roll up her sleeves and get to (spiritual) work.

But how? What should we do to help our directee prepare for desolation? What follows are four concrete things we can do. The first two are easy and straightforward. The second two are difficult and labor intensive.

- **Encourage humility.** Ignatius says that one of the reasons God allows us to experience desolation is to show us that we are not the source of our own consolation.[50] From this we can infer that the false spirit tries to sabotage our consolation by getting us to believe that we ourselves brought about our own consolation: "Aren't I good? Holy? Clever?" To prevent the onset of this pride, we can encourage our directee to humbly give God the glory, to praise and thank God for this *undeserved gift* of consolation. Reminding the directee of this susceptibility to pride might help her move toward greater humility.

- **Encourage journaling about the experience of consolation.** Early in my spiritual life, I found that I tended to journal only in times of desolation. When times were good, I didn't write a word! But by journaling during consolation, I am providing myself with *written evidence* of the veracity of the experience for when the storms of desolation return. In desolation, I tend to doubt whether the previous consolation was "real" or whether I was "just making that stuff up." But if I have a previous journal entry from a time of consolation to prove that "this really happened—it's here in black and white," then it is harder for me to deny its veracity.

- **Together, debrief the past experience of desolation.** Ignatius puts it well:

  When the enemy of our human nature has been detected and recognized by the trail of evil marking his course and by the wicked end to which he leads us, it will be profitable for one who has been tempted to review immediately the whole course of the temptation. Let him consider the series of good thoughts, how they arose, how the evil one gradually attempted to make him step down from the state of spiritual delight and joy in which he was, till finally he drew him to his wicked designs. The purpose of this review is that once such an experience has been understood and carefully observed, we may guard ourselves for the future against the customary deceits of the enemy.[51]

How is it that we humans have come to the point of so few accidental commercial plane crashes? It's simple: over the decades, after each crash we have recovered the "black boxes" that have meticulously recorded every moment of the ill-fated flight, from the preparations, through the takeoff, to the moment of the crash. The experts carefully study every tiny bit of every recorded datum. From this experience, they can usually diagnose the problem and work on a preventative solution. We should do the same with desolation. Once we have recovered from our "crash," we should extract the "black boxes" of data about the experience in order to diagnose the contributing factors and work on preventative solutions. Like scientists, the directee and I can investigate "the beginning and middle and end of the course":[52]

The Beginning

1. When did the desolation begin?
2. What were the external events and internal thoughts and feelings that preceded the desolation?
3. How did my interior self step from the previous consolation into the desolation?

The Middle

1. When in the midst of desolation, what things did I do, say, or think that helped me think and feel better?

2. What things did I do, say, or think that made the experience worse?

3. What were the lies and twisted truths being proposed to me by the false spirit?

The End

1. When exactly did the desolation end? What external events and/or internal thoughts or feelings led into the experience of coming out of the desolation?

2. How did my interior self step forward into consolation?

3. How did I prevail against the lies and twisted truths? Were there any providential truths that I clung to as I moved out of the desolation?

- **Help the directee fortify the holes in the fortress walls.** Again, let's turn to Ignatius for wisdom:

> The conduct of our enemy may also be compared to the tactics of a leader intent upon seizing and plundering a position he desires. A commander and leader of an army will encamp, explore the fortifications and defenses of the stronghold, and attack at the weakest point. In the same way, the enemy of our human nature investigates from every side all our virtues, theological, cardinal and moral. Where he finds the defenses of eternal salvation weakest and most deficient, there he attacks and tries to take us by storm.[53]

The false spirit is not very creative or innovative. Time and again, it attacks us in the very same "places" in our souls and psyches. This is great news for us! If we discover and fortify those spots while we're in the empowering moments of consolation, then the false spirit will have a tougher time getting through that "weakest point" the next time. So, while in consolation, the directee could explore these questions:

- What are my sinful inclinations? What are the roots of my sins? This is a different exploration than the one we do when preparing for the sacrament of reconciliation. Here, we're not so interested in the infractions themselves but rather in the root causes of the infractions (a tendency toward fear, anger, pride).
- What are the "buttons" that, when pushed, set me off on a crash course? About which topics or issues am I sensitive?
- What unhealthy coping mechanisms (psychologists would call them defense mechanisms) do I tend to employ (repression, aggression, passive-aggression, withdrawal)?

Notes

Notes

17

Accompanying Someone through Consolation without Previous Cause

Let's recall our working definition of this experience: Earlier I proposed that consolation without previous cause is the spiritual experience wherein the intensity of consolation we experience is far out of proportion to the preceding cause.[54] These are the spontaneous moments when God—for no clear reason—gives us a Big Kiss. God gives us an almost overwhelming experience of consoling joy that seems way out of proportion to any joy-inducing thing that is happening to us at the moment.

How should I, as a spiritual director or pastoral counselor, accompany someone who is experiencing this Big Kiss?

Several of the instructions throughout this book about accompanying someone through regular consolation apply well for this special consolation. Three of those instructions are particularly good for this experience:

I stay out of the way.

This is clearly an intimate moment between my directee and God. Therefore, the director should err on the side of backing up from the experience rather than interfering.

I encourage the directee to relish the experience.

You can, however, contribute to the experience by encouraging the directee to joyfully recount this extraordinary moment. Having to tell the director all about it will help the directee to marvel in wonder, asking, "Wasn't my heart burning inside me as I met God on the road?"

I encourage journaling the experience.

The directee will want to draw on this experience in the future, especially during difficult times.

In addition to these instructions borrowed from those for accompanying regular consolation, I would add two more:

I look out for and discourage overanalyzing.

This extraordinary experience is about as close as we can get to a transcendent moment with God. Trying to capture the experience by intellectually grasping exactly what happened, why it happened, and so forth might actually cheapen the experience. A friend and I used to have a saying about this. When one of us was sharing a deep moment of consolation that seemed to be of this "without cause" nature and would then begin to overanalyze the experience, the other would say, "Don't scribble on the altar." That was code for "Hey, buddy, just enjoy the sacred moment—enjoy the Big Kiss." We see this happening to Peter at the Transfiguration. After this experience of a lifetime:

> Peter said to Jesus, "Master, it is good that we are here; let us make three tents, one for you, one for Moses, and one for Elijah." But he did not know what he was saying. (Luke 9:33)

After the experience of consolation without previous cause, we, like Peter, know not what we are saying. When we try to "make three tents"—that is, build a shrine to our consolation—we tend to spoil the moment and we sound a little loopy. Better not to scribble on the altar but rather to hush and to relish the Big Kiss.

I encourage caution about the time just after this experience, especially regarding making decisions and taking action.

As I thoroughly presented earlier, the vulnerability of the experience could leave us vulnerable to other influences that do not wish us well.[55] We must be careful when coming down from the mountaintop "high" of this experience.

Notes

Notes

PART THREE

RESOURCES HELPFUL TO SPIRITUAL DIRECTORS, PASTORAL COUNSELORS, AND OTHER SPIRITUAL HELPERS

Resource #1: Rules for Discernment of Spirits—Primary Text

Rules for the Discernment of Spirits[56]

The First Week

Rules for understanding to some extent the different movements produced in the soul and for recognizing those that are good to admit them, and those that are bad, to reject them. These rules are more suited to the first week.

I. (314)

In the case of those who go from one mortal sin to another, the enemy is ordinarily accustomed to propose apparent pleasures. He fills their imagination with sensual delights and gratifications, the more readily to keep them in their vices and increase the number of their sins.

With such persons the good spirit uses a method which is the reverse of the above. Making use of the light of reason, he will rouse the sting of conscience and fill them with remorse.

II. (315)

In the case of those who go on earnestly striving to cleanse their souls from sin and who seek to rise in the service of God our Lord to greater perfection, the method pursued is the opposite of that mentioned in the first rule.

Then it is characteristic of the evil spirit to harass with anxiety, to afflict with sadness, to raise obstacles backed by fallacious reasonings that disturb the soul. Thus he seeks to prevent the soul from advancing.

It is characteristic of the good spirit, however, to give courage and strength, consolations, tears, inspirations, and peace. This He does by making all easy, by removing all obstacles so that the soul goes forward in doing good.

III. (316)

Spiritual Consolation. I call it consolation when an interior movement is aroused in the soul, by which it is inflamed with love of its Creator and Lord, and as a consequence, can love no creature on the face of the earth for its own sake, but only in the Creator of them all. It is likewise consolation when one sheds tears that move to the love of God, whether it be because of sorrow for sins, or because of the sufferings of Christ our Lord, or for any other reason that is immediately directed to the praise and service of God. Finally, I call consolation every increase of faith, hope, and love, and all interior joy that invites and attracts to what is heavenly and to the salvation of one's soul by filling it with peace and quiet in its Creator and Lord.

IV. (317)

Spiritual Desolation. I call desolation what is entirely the opposite of what is described in the third rule, as darkness of soul, turmoil of spirit, inclination to what is low and earthly, restlessness rising from many disturbances and temptations which lead to want of faith, want of hope, want of love. The soul is wholly slothful, tepid, sad, and separated, as it were, from its Creator and Lord. For just as consolation is the opposite of desolation, so the thoughts that spring from consolation are the opposite of those that spring from desolation.

V. (318)

In time of desolation we should never make any change, but remain firm and constant in the resolution and decision which guided us the day before the desolation, or in the decision to which we adhered in the preceding consolation. For just as in consolation the good spirit guides and counsels us, so in desolation the evil spirit guides and counsels. Following his counsels we can never find the way to a right decision.

VI. (319)

Though in desolation we must never change our former resolutions, it will be very advantageous to intensify our activity against the desolation. We can insist more upon prayer, upon meditation, and on much examination of ourselves. We can make an effort in a suitable way to do some penance.

VII. (320)

When one is in desolation, he should be mindful that God has left him to his natural powers to resist the different agitations and temptations of the enemy in order to try him. He can resist with the help of God, which always remains, though he may not clearly perceive it. For though God has taken from him the abundance of fervor and overflowing love and the intensity of His favors, nevertheless, he has sufficient grace for eternal salvation.

VIII. (321)

When one is in desolation, he should strive to persevere in patience. This reacts against the vexations that have overtaken him. Let him consider, too, that consolation will soon return, and in the meantime, he must diligently use the means against desolation which have been given in the sixth rule.

IX. (322)

The principal reasons why we suffer from desolation are three:

The first is because we have been tepid and slothful or negligent in our exercises of piety, and so through our own fault spiritual consolation has been taken away from us.

The second reason is because God wishes to try us, to see how much we are worth, and how much we will advance in His service and praise when left without the generous reward of consolations and signal favors.

The third reason is because God wishes to give us a true knowledge and understanding of ourselves, so that we may have an intimate perception of the fact that it is not within our power to acquire and attain great devotion, intense love, tears, or any other spiritual consolation; but that all this is the gift and grace of God our Lord. God does not wish us to build on the property of another, to rise up in spirit in a certain pride and vainglory and attribute to ourselves the devotion and other effects of spiritual consolation.

X. (323)

When one enjoys consolation, let him consider how he will
conduct himself during the time of ensuing desolation,
and store up a supply of strength as defense against
that day.

XI. (324)

He who enjoys consolation should take care to humble
himself and lower himself as much as possible. Let him
recall how little he is able to do in time of desolation, when
he is left without such grace or consolation.

On the other hand, one who suffers desolation should
remember that by making use of the sufficient grace
offered him, he can do much to withstand all his enemies.
Let him find his strength in his Creator and Lord.

XII. (325)

The enemy conducts himself as a woman. He is a weakling
before a show of strength, and a tyrant if he has his will. It
is characteristic of a woman in a quarrel with a man to lose
courage and take to flight if the man shows that he is
determined and fearless. However, if the man loses courage
and begins to flee, the anger, vindictiveness, and rage of the
woman surge up and know no bounds. In the same way,
the enemy becomes weak, loses courage, and turns to flight
with his seductions as soon as one leading a spiritual life
faces his temptations boldly, and does exactly the opposite
of what he suggests. However, if one begins to be afraid
and to lose courage in temptations, no wild animal on
earth can be more fierce than the enemy of our human
nature. He will carry out his perverse intentions with consummate malice.[57]

XIII. (326)

Our enemy may also be compared in his manner of acting to a false lover. He seeks to remain hidden and does not want to be discovered. If such a lover speaks with evil intention to the daughter of a good father, or to the wife of a good husband, and seeks to seduce them, he wants his words and solicitations kept secret. He is greatly displeased if his evil suggestions and depraved intentions are revealed by the daughter to her father, or by the wife to her husband. Then he readily sees he will not succeed in what he has begun. In the same way, when the enemy of our human nature tempts a just soul with his wiles and seductions, he earnestly desires that they be received secretly and kept secret. But if one manifests them to a confessor, or to some other spiritual person who understands his deceits and malicious designs, the evil one is very much vexed. For he knows that he cannot succeed in his evil undertaking, once his evident deceits have been revealed.

XIV. (327)

The conduct of our enemy may also be compared to the tactics of a leader intent upon seizing and plundering a position he desires. A commander and leader of an army will encamp, explore the fortifications and defenses of the stronghold, and attack at the weakest point. In the same way, the enemy of our human nature investigates from every side all our virtues, theological, cardinal and moral. Where he finds the defenses of eternal salvation weakest and most deficient, there he attacks and tries to take us by storm.

(328)

The Second Week

Further rules for understanding the different movements produced in the soul. They serve for a more accurate discernment of spirits and are more suitable for the second week.

I. (329)

It is characteristic of God and His Angels, when they act upon the soul, to give true happiness and spiritual joy, and to banish all the sadness and disturbances which are caused by the enemy.

It is characteristic of the evil one to fight against such happiness and consolation by proposing fallacious reasonings, subtleties, and continual deceptions.

II. (330)

God alone can give consolation to the soul without any previous cause. It belongs solely to the Creator to come into a soul, to leave it, to act upon it, to draw it wholly to the love of His Divine Majesty. I said without previous cause, that is, without any preceding perception or knowledge of any subject by which a soul might be led to such a consolation through its own acts of intellect and will.

III. (331)

If a cause precedes, both the good angel and the evil spirit can give consolation to a soul, but for a quite different purpose. The good angel consoles for the progress of the soul, that it may advance and rise to what is more perfect. The evil spirit consoles for purposes that are the contrary, and that afterwards he might draw the soul to his own perverse intentions and wickedness.

IV. (332)

It is a mark of the evil spirit to assume the appearance of an angel of light. He begins by suggesting thoughts that are suited to a devout soul, and ends by suggesting his own. For example, he will suggest holy and pious thoughts that are wholly in conformity with the sanctity of the soul. Afterwards, he will endeavor little by little to end by drawing the soul into his hidden snares and evil designs.

V. (333)

We must carefully observe the whole course of our thoughts. If the beginning and middle and end of the course of thoughts are wholly good and directed to what is entirely right, it is a sign that they are from the good angel. But the course of thoughts suggested to us may terminate in something evil, or distracting, or less good than the soul had formerly proposed to do. Again, it may end in what weakens the soul, or disquiets it; or by destroying the peace, tranquillity, and quiet which it had before, it may cause disturbance to the soul. These things are a clear sign that the thoughts are proceeding from the evil spirit, the enemy of our progress and eternal salvation.

VI. (334)

When the enemy of our human nature has been detected and recognized by the trail of evil marking his course and by the wicked end to which he leads us, it will be profitable for one who has been tempted to review immediately the whole course of the temptation. Let him consider the series of good thoughts, how they arose, how the evil one gradually attempted to make him step down from the state of spiritual delight and joy in which he was, till finally he drew him to his wicked designs. The purpose of this review is that once such an experience has been understood and carefully observed, we may guard ourselves for the future against the customary deceits of the enemy.

VII. (335)

In souls that are progressing to greater perfection, the action of the good angel is delicate, gentle, delightful. It may be compared to a drop of water penetrating a sponge.

The action of the evil spirit upon such souls is violent, noisy, and disturbing. It may be compared to a drop of water falling upon a stone.

In souls that are going from bad to worse, the action of the spirits mentioned above is just the reverse. The reason for this is to be sought in the opposition or similarity of these souls to the different kinds of spirits. When the disposition is contrary to that of the spirits, they enter with noise and commotion that are easily perceived. When the disposition is similar to that of the spirits, they enter silently, as one coming into his own house when the doors are open.

VIII. (336)

When consolation is without previous cause, as was said, there can be no deception in it, since it can proceed from God our Lord only. But a spiritual person who has received such a consolation must consider it very attentively, and must cautiously distinguish the actual time of the consolation from the period which follows it. At such a time the soul is still fervent and favored with the grace and aftereffects of the consolation which has passed. In this second period the soul frequently forms various resolutions and plans which are not granted directly by God our Lord. They may come from our own reasoning on the relations of our concepts and on the consequences of our judgments, or they may come from the good or evil spirit. Hence, they must be carefully examined before they are given full approval and put into execution.

Notes

Notes

Resource #2: Everything Ignatius Said About . . .

Everything Ignatius Said about Desolation and How the Evil Spirit Acts on the Soul

—In the case of those who go from one mortal sin to another, the enemy is ordinarily accustomed to propose apparent pleasures. He fills their imagination with sensual delights and gratifications, the more readily to keep them in their vices and increase the number of their sins. (Rule 1, First Week)

—In the case of those who go on earnestly striving to cleanse their souls from sin and who seek to rise in the service of God our Lord to greater perfection . . . it is characteristic of the evil spirit to harass with anxiety, to afflict with sadness, to raise obstacles backed by fallacious reasonings that disturb the soul. Thus he seeks to prevent the soul from advancing. (Rule 2, First Week)

—I call desolation . . . darkness of soul, turmoil of spirit, inclination to what is low and earthly, restlessness rising from many disturbances and temptations which lead to want of faith, want of hope, want of love. The soul is wholly slothful, tepid, sad, and separated, as it were, from its Creator and Lord. (Rule 4, First Week)

—In time of desolation we should never make any change, but remain firm and constant in the resolution and decision which guided us the day before the desolation, or in the decision to which we adhered in the preceding consolation. For just as in consolation the good spirit guides and counsels us, so in desolation the evil spirit guides and counsels. Following his counsels we can never find the way to a right decision. (Rule 5, First Week)

—Though in desolation we must never change our former resolutions, it will be very advantageous to intensify our activity against the desolation. We can insist more upon prayer, upon meditation, and on much examination of ourselves. We can make an effort in a suitable way to do some penance. (Rule 6, First Week)

—When one is in desolation, he should be mindful that God has left him to his natural powers to resist the different agitations and temptations of the enemy in order to try him. He can resist with the help of God, which always remains, though he may not clearly perceive it. For though God has taken from him the abundance of fervor and overflowing love and the intensity of His favors, nevertheless, he has sufficient grace for eternal salvation. (Rule 7, First Week)

—When one is in desolation, he should strive to persevere in patience. This reacts against the vexations that have overtaken him. Let him consider, too, that consolation will soon return, and in the meantime, he must diligently use the means against desolation which have been given in the sixth rule. (Rule 8, First Week)

—The principal reasons why we suffer from desolation are three:

The first is because we have been tepid and slothful or negligent in our exercises of piety, and so through our own fault spiritual consolation has been taken away from us.

The second reason is because God wishes to try us, to see how much we are worth, and how much we will advance in His service and praise when left without the generous reward of consolations and signal favors.

The third reason is because God wishes to give us a true knowledge and understanding of ourselves, so that we may have an intimate perception of the fact that it is not within our power to acquire and attain great devotion, intense love, tears, or any other spiritual consolation; but that all this is the gift and grace of God our Lord. God does not wish us to build on the property of another, to rise up in spirit in a certain pride and vainglory and attribute to ourselves the devotion and other effects of spiritual consolation. (Rule 9, First Week)

—One who suffers desolation should remember that by making use of the sufficient grace offered him, he can do much to withstand all his enemies. Let him find his strength in his Creator and Lord. (Rule 11, First Week)

—The enemy conducts himself as a woman. He is a weakling before a show of strength, and a tyrant if he has his will.

It is characteristic of a woman in a quarrel with a man to lose courage and take to flight if the man shows that he is determined and fearless. However, if the man loses courage and begins to flee, the anger, vindictiveness, and rage of the woman surge up and know no bounds. In the same way, the enemy becomes weak, loses courage, and turns to flight with his seductions as soon as one leading a spiritual life faces his temptations boldly, and does exactly the opposite of what he suggests. However, if one begins to be afraid and to lose courage in temptations, no wild animal on earth can be more fierce than the enemy of our human nature. He will carry out his perverse intentions with consummate malice. (Rule 12, First Week)[58]

—Our enemy may also be compared in his manner of acting to a false lover. He seeks to remain hidden and does not want to be discovered. If such a lover speaks with evil intention to the daughter of a good father, or to the wife of a good husband, and seeks to seduce them, he wants his words and solicitations kept secret. He is greatly displeased if his evil suggestions and depraved intentions are revealed by the daughter to her father, or by the wife to her husband. Then he readily sees he will not succeed in what he has begun. In the same way, when the enemy of our human nature tempts a just soul with his wiles and seductions, he earnestly desires that they be received secretly and kept secret. But if one manifests them to a confessor, or to some other spiritual person who understands his deceits and malicious designs, the evil one is very much vexed. For he knows that he cannot succeed in his evil undertaking, once his evident deceits have been revealed. (Rule 13, First Week)

—The conduct of our enemy may also be compared to the tactics of a leader intent upon seizing and plundering a position he desires. A commander and leader of an army will encamp, explore the fortifications and defenses of the stronghold, and attack at the weakest point. In the same way, the enemy of our human nature investigates from every side all our virtues, theological, cardinal and moral. Where he finds the defenses of eternal salvation weakest and most deficient, there he attacks and tries to take us by storm. (Rule 14, First Week)

—It is characteristic of the evil one to fight against . . . happiness and consolation by proposing fallacious reasonings, subtleties, and continual deceptions. (Rule 1, Second Week)

—The evil spirit consoles for [these] purposes . . . that afterwards he might draw the soul to his own perverse intentions and wickedness. (Rule 3, Second Week)

—It is a mark of the evil spirit to assume the appearance of an angel of light. He begins by suggesting thoughts that are suited to a devout soul, and ends by suggesting his own. For example, he will suggest holy and pious thoughts that are wholly in conformity with the sanctity of the soul. Afterwards, he will endeavor little by little to end by drawing the soul into his hidden snares and evil designs. (Rule 4, Second Week)

—We must carefully observe the whole course of our thoughts. . . . The beginning and middle and end of the course of thoughts . . . may terminate in something evil, or distracting, or less good than the soul had formerly proposed to do. Again, it may end in what weakens the soul, or disquiets it; or by destroying the peace, tranquility, and quiet which it had before, it may cause disturbance to the soul. These things are a clear sign that the thoughts are proceeding from the evil spirit, the enemy of our progress and eternal salvation. (Rule 5, Second Week)

—When the enemy of our human nature has been detected and recognized by the trail of evil marking his course and by the wicked end to which he leads us, it will be profitable for one who has been tempted to review immediately the whole course of the temptation. Let him consider the series of good thoughts, how they arose, how the evil one gradually attempted to make him step down from the state of spiritual delight and joy in which he was, till finally he drew him to his wicked designs. The purpose of this review is that once such an experience has been understood and carefully observed, we may guard ourselves for the future against the customary deceits of the enemy. (Rule 6, Second Week)

—In souls that are progressing to greater perfection, the action of the good angel is delicate, gentle, delightful. It may be compared to a drop of water penetrating a sponge.

The action of the evil spirit upon such souls is violent, noisy, and disturbing. It may be compared to a drop of water falling upon a stone.

In souls that are going from bad to worse, the action of the spirits mentioned above is just the reverse. The reason for this is to be sought in the opposition or similarity of these souls to the different kinds of spirits. When the disposition is contrary to that of the spirits, they enter with noise and commotion that are easily perceived. When the disposition is similar to that of the spirits, they enter silently, as one coming into his own house when the doors are open. (Rule 7, Second Week)

—When the [director perceives that the directee is in placid desolation], he ought to ply him with questions about [his spiritual practices]. He should ask him whether he makes them at the appointed times, and how he makes them. He should question . . . whether he is diligent in the observance of them. He will demand an account in detail of each one of these points. (Annotation #6, Introductory Observations)

—If the director . . . observes that the [directee] is in desolation and tempted, let him not deal severely and harshly with him, but gently and kindly. He should encourage and strengthen him for the future by exposing to him the wiles of the enemy of our human nature, and by getting him to prepare and dispose himself for the coming consolation. (Annotation #7, Introductory Observations)

—[The directee] must always take care that he is satisfied in the consciousness of having persevered in the exercise for a full [time to which he has committed]. Let him rather exceed [rather] than not use the full time. . . . For the enemy is accustomed to make every effort that the [amount of time to which the directee has committed] to be devoted to a contemplation, meditation, or prayer should be shortened. (Annotation #12, Introductory Observations)

—We must remember that during the time of consolation it is easy, and requires only a slight effort, to continue a whole [time committed] in contemplation, but in time of desolation it is very difficult to do so. Hence, in order to fight against the desolation and conquer the temptation, the [directee] must always remain in the exercise a little more than the [time committed]. Thus he will accustom himself not only to resist the enemy, but even to overthrow him. [In the Ignatian world of spiritual direction, we call this concept *agere contra* (to act against). So, for example, if we have committed ourselves to thirty minutes of prayer and are tempted one day to "trim" it back to twenty-five minutes, we will—on that day—pray for thirty-five minutes as an act of *agere contra*. Thus, we will purposely overcompensate for our temptations to skimp on our spiritual commitments. This practice of *agere contra* can be applied to any of our spiritual commitments.] (Annotation #13, Introductory Observations)

—[To speak a little more about *agere contra*,] the Creator and Lord may work with greater certainty in His creature, if the soul chance to be inordinately attached or inclined to anything, it is very proper that it rouse itself by the exertion of all its powers to desire the opposite of that to which it is wrongly attached. Thus if one's attachment leads him to seek and to hold an office or a benefice, not for the honor and glory of God our Lord, nor for the spiritual welfare of souls, but for his own personal gain and temporal interests, he should strive to rouse a desire for the contrary. Let him be insistent in prayer and in his other spiritual exercises in begging God for the reverse, that is, that he neither seek such office or benefice, nor anything else, unless the Divine Majesty duly regulate his desires and change his former attachment. As a result, the reason he wants or retains any-thing will be solely the service, honor, and glory of the Divine Majesty. (Annotation #16, Introductory Observations)

Everything Ignatius Said about Consolation and How the Good Spirit Acts on the Soul

—In the case of those who go from one mortal sin to another . . . the good spirit uses a method which is the reverse of [the evil spirit]. Making use of the light of reason, he will rouse the sting of conscience and fill them with remorse. (Rule 1, First Week)

—In the case of those who go on earnestly striving to cleanse their souls from sin and who seek to rise in the service of God our Lord to greater perfection . . . it is characteristic of the good spirit . . . to give courage and strength, consolations, tears, inspirations, and peace. This He does by making all easy, by removing all obstacles so that the soul goes forward in doing good. (Rule 2, First Week)

—*Spiritual Consolation.* I call it consolation when an interior movement is aroused in the soul, by which it is inflamed with love of its Creator and Lord, and as a consequence, can love no creature on the face of the earth for its own sake, but only in the Creator of them all. It is likewise consolation when one sheds tears that move to the love of God, whether it be because of sor-row for sins, or because of the sufferings of Christ our Lord, or for any other reason that is immediately directed to the praise and service of God. Finally, I call consolation every increase of faith, hope, and love, and all interior joy that invites and attracts to what is heavenly and to the salvation of one's soul by filling it with peace and quiet in its Creator and Lord. (Rule 3, First Week)

—When one enjoys consolation, let him consider how he will conduct himself during the time of ensuing desolation, and store up a supply of strength as defense against that day. (Rule 10, First Week)

—He who enjoys consolation should take care to humble himself and lower himself as much as possible. Let him recall how little he is able to do in time of desolation, when he is left without such grace or consolation. (Rule 11, First Week)

—It is characteristic of God and His Angels, when they act upon the soul, to give true happiness and spiritual joy, and to banish all the sadness and disturbances which are caused by the enemy. (Rule 1, Second Week)

—The good angel consoles for the progress of the soul, that it may advance and rise to what is more perfect. (Rule 3, Second Week)

—We must carefully observe the whole course of our thoughts. [Only] if the beginning and middle and end of the course of thoughts are wholly good and directed to what is entirely right, it is a sign that they are from the good angel. (Rule 5, Second Week)

—[The good spirit will treat souls differently depending on whether the soul (a) is in sync with God, progressing to greater perfection, or (b) is not in sync with God, going from bad to worse.]

In souls that are progressing to greater perfection, the action of the good angel is delicate, gentle, delightful. It may be compared to a drop of water penetrating a sponge.

In souls that are going from bad to worse, [the action of the good angel is violent, noisy, and disturbing. It may be compared to a drop of water falling upon a stone].

The reason for this is to be sought in the opposition or similarity of these souls to the different kinds of spirits. When the disposition is contrary to that of the spirits, they enter with noise and commotion that are easily perceived. When the disposition is similar to that of the spirits, they enter silently, as one coming into his own house when the doors are open. (Rule 7, Second Week)

—If the [director] sees that the [directee] is going on in consolation and in great fervor, he must admonish him not to be inconsiderate or hasty in making any promise or vow. The more unstable in character he knows him to be, the more he should forewarn and admonish him. [By resisting a hasty vow, he will have avoided the temptation of moving from true consolation to false consolation.] (Annotation #14, Introductory Observations)

Everything Ignatius Said about Consolation without Previous Cause

—God alone can give consolation to the soul without any previous cause. It belongs solely to the Creator to come into a soul, to leave it, to act upon it, to draw it wholly to the love of His Divine Majesty. I said without previous cause, that is, without any preceding perception or knowledge of any subject by which a soul might be led to such a consolation through its own acts of intellect and will. (Rule 2, Second Week)

—When consolation is without previous cause, as was said, there can be no deception in it, since it can proceed from God our Lord only. But a spiritual person who has received such a consolation must consider it very attentively, and must cautiously distinguish the actual time of the consolation from the period which follows it. At such a time the soul is still fervent and favored with the grace and aftereffects of the consolation which has passed. In this second period the soul frequently forms various resolutions and plans which are not granted directly by God our Lord. They may come from our own reasoning on the relations of our concepts and on the consequences of our judgments, or they may come from the good or evil spirit. Hence, they must be carefully examined before they are given full approval and put into execution. (Rule 8, Second Week)

—If the one who is giving the Exercises sees that the exercitant [the directee] is going on in consolation and in great fervor, he must admonish him not to be inconsiderate or hasty in making any promise or vow. The more unstable in character he knows him to be, the more he should forewarn and admonish him. For though it is right to urge one to enter the religious state in which he knows that vows of obedience, poverty, and chastity are taken, and though a good work done under vow is more meritorious than one done without a vow, nevertheless, it is necessary to consider with great care the condition and endowments of each individual, and the help or hindrance one would experience in carrying out his promises. (Annotation #14)[59]

Notes

Notes

Resource #3: Suggested Scripture Passages

Consolation and Consolation without Previous Cause

Psalm 8	"What is man that you should care for him?"
Psalm 27	"The Lord is my light and my salvation."
Psalm 62	"My soul rests in God alone."
Psalm 63:1–9	"All through the night I will meditate on you."
Psalm 103	"Bless the Lord, O my soul."
Psalm 104	"Praise the Lord, O my soul."
Psalm 116	"What return shall I make for the good He has done for me?"
Psalm 122	"I rejoiced when I heard them say . . ."
Psalm 139	"I praise you, I am wonderfully made; wonderful are your works!"
Psalm 145	"One generation shall laud your works to another."
Psalm 149:1–5	"Praise him with dancing, making melody with tambourine."
Sirach 14:11–16	"Enjoy your good life."
Isaiah 43	"You are precious in my eyes and I love you."
Jeremiah 1:4–10	"Before I formed you, I knew you."
Daniel 3:52–90	"All things bless the lord."
Matthew 13:44–45	The pearl of great price
Luke 1:26–38	"Here am I, the servant of the Lord."

Luke 1:39–45	"My soul magnifies the Lord."
Luke 5:33–39	Celebrate while the bridegroom is with you.
Luke 17:11–19	The grateful leper
Luke 24:13–35	The resurrected Jesus on the road to Emmaus
John 10:1–21	Jesus is the Good Shepherd; he knows my name.
John 15:9–17	"That your joy may be complete."
Acts 2:1–13	The Holy Spirit descends upon them, and they are sent out.
Romans 8:28–39	All things work together for the good.
1 Corinthians 1:4–9	You lack no spiritual gift.
1 Corinthians 2:6–16	"Eye has not seen; ears have not heard."
2 Corinthians 9:6–15	"God loves a cheerful giver."
Philippians 1:3–26	"I thank God every time I remember you."
Philippians 4:4–13	"Rejoice in the Lord, always."
Colossians 1:3–20	"By Him, all things were created."
2 Timothy 4:6–8	"I have run the good race."
1 Peter 3:8–17	"Be prepared to give an account for the hope that is in you."
Revelation 21:1–5	"Behold, I make all things new."

False Consolation

2 Samuel 7:1–13	David thinks he will provide for God. God corrects him.
Psalm 127:1–2	Unless the Lord builds the house, those who build it labor in vain.
Ecclesiastes 4:1–4	All is vanity and a striving after wind.
Isaiah 30:15–21	By waiting you shall be saved; in quiet your strength lies.
Mark 10:17–25	Jesus invites the rich young man to follow him.
Luke 10:38–42	Martha is serving Jesus when Jesus is calling her to spend time with him.
Luke 18:9–14	The publican and the Pharisee

John 11:45–52	The Pharisees think they are doing God's will by plotting against Jesus.
John 13:1–20	Jesus washes his disciples' feet.
Acts 9:9–19	Saul (Paul) thinks he is being a good servant of God by persecuting Christians. Christ shows him his blindness and makes him see.
1 Peter 5:8–9	Be sober and alert.
Psalm 46:9–12	"Be still and know that I am God."
1 John 1:5–10	"If we say that we have no sin, we deceive ourselves."

Desolation and Difficult Consolation

Numbers 11:10–15	Lord, why have you treated me so badly?
Judith 8:25–27	Not for vengeance did the Lord test them.
Job 7:11–19	"I will complain in the bitterness of my soul."
Job 19:23–27	"I know that my Redeemer lives."
Psalm 6	Prayer in time of distress
Psalm 13	"How long will you hide your face from me?"
Psalm 22	"My God, why have you forsaken me?"
Psalm 23	"The Lord is my shepherd; I shall want for nothing."
Psalm 42	"My soul is cast down within me."
Psalm 51	"Wash me, O Lord."
Psalm 69	"Save me, O God."
Psalm 86	"Give ear, O Lord, to my prayer."
Psalm 88	"Lord, my soul is full of troubles."
Psalm 91	"He will rescue you from the snare of the fowler."
Psalm 102	"I am withered, dried up like the grass."
Psalm 118	"The Lord is with me; I fear not."
Psalm 126	"They shall return rejoicing."
Psalm 131	"I have calmed and quieted my soul."

Psalm 137:1–6	"How could we sing the Lord's song in a foreign land?"
Psalm 143:6–7	"My soul thirsts for you."
Ecclesiastes 3:1–8	"There is a time to laugh and a time to mourn."
Sirach 2:1–11	Proper disposition during adversity
Isaiah 2:2–5	"They shall beat their swords into plowshares."
Isaiah 43:1–8	"When you walk through fire, you shall not be burned."
Isaiah 43:14–21	"See, I am doing something new."
Isaiah 49:1–18	"See, upon the palms of my hands I've written your name."
Isaiah 55:1–13	"All who are thirsty, come to the water."
Isaiah 64	"O, that you would rend the heavens and come down!"
Jeremiah 18	The potter
Jeremiah 20:7–18	"You duped me, O Lord."
Jeremiah 29:11–13	"I have plans of goodness for you."
Lamentations 3	"I am a man who has seen affliction."
Ezekiel 37:1–14	God brings dry bones to life.
Matthew 6:25–34	"Stop worrying; the Father knows your needs."
Matthew 10:26–33	God has counted every hair on your head.
Matthew 11:28–30	"Come to me, all you who are weary."
Matthew 19:27–30	All who have given up will receive.
Matthew 23:37–39	Jesus weeps over Jerusalem.
Mark 4:35–41	Jesus calms the storm.
Mark 9:14–29	"I do believe; help my unbelief."
Mark 14:32–42	Agony in the garden: "Remove this cup from me."
Mark 15:33–34	"My God, why have you forsaken me?"
Luke 4:16–21	"The Spirit of the Lord is upon me to comfort the mourning."
Luke 5:1–11	"We have fished all night and caught nothing."

Luke 6:20–23	"Blessed are you who weep now, for you will laugh."
Luke 7:11–17	Jesus raises a widow's son.
Luke 8:49–56	Jesus raises the daughter of Jairus.
Luke 10:38–42	"Martha, Martha, you are anxious about many things."
Luke 11:5–13	If one keeps knocking, the master arises.
Luke 22:40–46	Jesus sweats blood in the Garden of Gethsemane.
John 5:1–16	The man at the pool of Bethesda
John 11:1–44	Jesus raises Lazarus.
John 12:23–25	"Unless a grain of wheat falls to the ground . . ."
John 14:1–3	"In my Father's house there are many dwelling places."
John 16:33	You will suffer, but take courage.
John 20:19–29	Doubting Thomas
Romans 5:1–5	"We exult in our tribulations."
Romans 7:14–25	"What I want to do, I do not do."
Romans 8:26–39	"What can separate us from the love of Christ?"
1 Corinthians 15:50–57	"O death, where is your victory?"
2 Corinthians 1:3–5	"For as our sufferings are abundant, so is our consolation."
2 Corinthians 4:7–18	"We are afflicted but not crushed."
2 Corinthians 12:7–10	A thorn in my flesh; three times I begged for healing.
Ephesians 4:25–32	"Be kind to one another."
Colossians 1:22–29	"In my flesh I fill up what is lacking in the sufferings of Christ."
Hebrews 11:1–3	"Faith is the assurance of things hoped for."
Hebrews 12:5–13	"Strengthen your drooping hands and weak knees."
James 1:2–7	"The testing of your faith produces endurance."
1 Peter 1:3–9	"You may have to suffer for a time."

| 1 Peter 5:6–11 | "Cast all your cares on him, for he cares for you." |
| 1 John 4:18 | "Cast out all fear." |

Notes

Notes

Resource #4: Checklists to Assist in Determining Another Person's Spiritual State of Being

- In terms of **God's presence**, which statement seems to match the person's inner thoughts and feelings?

  - Consolation: "I feel God's presence strongly. I can easily and naturally 'taste and see' the effects of God's grace in my life."

  - Consolation without Previous Cause: "I'm overwhelmed by God's presence and love for me. Like Mary, 'My soul proclaims the greatness of the Lord. My spirit rejoices in God my savior, for God has looked with favor on his lowly servant.' I can't believe just how good God is and how much God loves me and the world. I have seldom felt so embraced by God. I want to sing of God's salvation."

  - Difficult Consolation: "I don't feel God's presence very strongly right now—which is disappointing and/or frustrating. But I know in my heart that God is present and that God loves me and is going to take care of me."

- Desolation: "I do not feel God's presence, and I am angry, discouraged, depressed, and/or hopeless about it. I know that I'm supposed to believe that God is there for me, but my heart just doesn't believe that right now."

- False Consolation: "God has anointed me to do God's work, and I'm determined to do it. I need to do it now, regardless of what other people think. If others do not perceive this divine experience I am having, it is because they simply are not able to grasp what I have grasped."

- In terms of **great desires for faith, hope, and love,** which statement seems to match the person's inner thoughts and feelings?

  - Consolation: "I feel great love for the people in my life, and I want to care for them as best I can. I am hopeful and optimistic that God will take care of me and of God's world, and I want to play a part in that providential care. I have a great desire to be loyal and faithful to my previous commitments and to the people whom God has sent me to be with."

  - Consolation without Previous Cause: "I'm swept up by love of God and of the people in my life. I love them so much! I desire nothing more than to be a loving person for them. It is extraordinarily easy for me to be good to them at this moment."

  - Difficult Consolation: "I don't feel the feelings of great love for this person or that person, but deeper down I do want to do God's will, and I am determined to do right by the people and commitments in my life. Despite my surface-level feelings, deeper down I feel peaceful, calm, and quiet."

○ Desolation: "I feel no great love for the very people that God has called me to love. I have no desire to be kind and generous toward them. I'm either lethargic about the good that I'm being asked to do or am downright resistant to being kind and loving. I feel myself pulling away from my loved ones. I'm even thinking of permanently pulling away. I find myself questioning the commitments that I've made in the past. When I think about my life and my relationships, I feel hopeless."

○ False Consolation: "God wants me to save this person or situation. Despite what the good and wise people in my life are saying, I need to do this radical, dramatic action, and I need to do it right now."

- The following are **descriptors** that the person uses in describing herself—or descriptors that you find yourself thinking while listening or when looking back on your conversation.

Consolation
desire to grow closer (to God and/or others)
easy to be faithful
emotionally strong
feeling loved and/or loving
grateful
happy
hopeful and optimistic

inspired toward generosity

open minded

sense God's presence

Consolation without Previous Cause

abundantly blessed

deep-down joy

deeply moved

"drunk" in the Spirit

ecstatic

inexplicable happiness

overwhelming gratitude

speechless with awe

swept off my feet

Difficult Consolation

committed

disappointed or sad but not depressed

emotionally stable

fortitude

hold the course

pensive

resolved

sober and realistic but not fatalistic

stay faithful

troubled but clearheaded

Desolation

all alone

anger or rage

anxiety or fear

boredom

critical (of self or others)

depressed

desire to get out, flee, sever relationships

despair

detached

fatalistic

fragile or unstable

hopeless

inconsolable

morbid

pessimistic

False Consolation

delusion

infatuated or obsessed (with a person or idea)

manic

me, me, me

naïve

over the top

overconfident

pollyannaish

radical inspiration

rash

unrealistic

unreflective

urgent

unstable

Notes

Notes

Resource #5: Glossary of Ignatian and Jesuit Terms

AMDG: Abbreviation for the Latin phrase *ad majorem Dei gloriam* or *ad maiorem Dei gloriam*. It means "to the greater glory of God." See *magis*.

Bad spirit: See *false spirit*.

Consolation: The inner state of being wherein the person is "in sync" with God and has great desires for faith, hope, and love.

Consolation without previous cause: The spiritual experience wherein the intensity of consolation we experience is far out of proportion to the preceding cause—or appears not to have a previous cause.

Desolation: The inner state of being wherein the person is "out of sync" with God and lacks great desires for faith, hope, and love.

Difficult consolation: The inner state of being wherein a person feels as though he or she is in desolation when in fact the person is in consolation.

Enemy of our human nature: See *false spirit*.

Evil spirit: See *false spirit.*

Examen (aka Ignatian Examen): An Ignatian way of praying wherein one devotes ten to fifteen minutes of prayer to reviewing one's day or half day, giving thanks for the good moments and seeking healing and/or forgiveness for the not-so-good ones. The prayer then concludes with looking ahead to the next half day or day, asking God for help to do God's will in particular ways.

False consolation: The inner state of being wherein the person feels as though they are in consolation when in fact they are in desolation.

False spirit (aka evil spirit, bad spirit, enemy of our human nature): While some would equate the evil spirit with the devil, I argue for a broader definition that would include but not be limited to the traditional understanding of evil. From the perspective of Ignatian spirituality, I would suggest that by "false spirit" we mean any spirit within us that moves us away from God and God's will.

Good spirit: While some would equate the good spirit with the Holy Spirit, I argue for a broader definition that would include but not be limited to the traditional understanding of the Holy Spirit. From the perspective of Ignatian spirituality, I would suggest that by "good spirit" we mean any movement within us that moves us toward God and God's will.

Ignatian Examen: See *Examen.*

Magis: Latin for "greater" or "more." A shorthand way of referring to the Ignatian idea of seeking not only the glory of God but even the *greater* glory of God. When we discern, we are working to decide "between goods," as Ignatius would say it, because there is no discernment when it comes to deciding between a good and a bad. Of course, we must always act toward the good. Therefore, in discerning between goods, we are attempting to come to know which choice will bring *greater* glory to God and will do *more* to build the kingdom of God on earth.

Praydreaming: The practice of daydreaming in the midst of one's prayer time. Discernment of choices often involves this imaginative exercise to help determine to which option God is calling the person.[60]

Rules for Election: A section of the *Spiritual Exercises*[61] wherein St. Ignatius describes three ways of coming to a prayerful decision (discernment). The first way is "without being able to doubt." The second way is through prayerful reasoning. The third way is through discerning the various movements and motivations within one's reflections.

Endnotes

1. The Rules for Discernment of Spirits can also be found in Resource #1 of this book. For more books delving into the subject, you could read my own introduction to Discernment of Spirits: *God's Voice Within* or Thomas Green's *Weeds Among the Wheat*. You could also read the numerous titles offered by Timothy Gallagher or Joseph Tetlow.

2. Some of these ideas have been proposed by scholars or practitioners long ago, and some have even been debated for centuries. When possible, I try to point the reader to earlier writings on the topic. However, since I am not a scholar myself, I have chosen to stick closer to my own personal reflections rather than to scholarship.

3. Rule 4, First Week, from *The Spiritual Exercises of St. Ignatius*, trans. Louis J. Puhl (Chicago: Loyola Press, 1951).

4. Rule 6, Second Week. In Fleming, *Draw Me Into Your Friendship*, Institute of Jesuit Sources, 1996, page 262.

5. Michael Palmer, SJ, ed. and trans., *On Giving the Spiritual Exercises* (1996), 86. http://jesuitsources.bc.edu/ on-giving-the-spiritual-exercises-the-early-jesuit-manuscript-directories-and-the -official-directory-of-1599/.

6. Annotation 13, Introductory Observations.

7. Palmer, 90.

8. Palmer, 301.

9. To be clear, the philosophical and theological questions about the nature of evil may be questions well worth exploring in spiritual direction. However, they are probably not the first topics you'll want to explore as you are introducing Ignatian discernment to your directee.

10. Rule 1, Second Week, Puhl.

11. Puhl, See Making a Choice of a Way of Life, paragraph #176.

12. For example, Timothy Gallagher, OMV, "the forms of awareness . . . psychological, moral, and spiritual." In his *The Discernment of Spirits* (Chestnut Ridge, NY: Crossroad, 2005), 20–23.

13. St. Ignatius of Loyola, *A Pilgrim's Testament: The Memoirs of St. Ignatius of Loyola*, transcribed by Luis Goncalves de Camara SJ, and translated by Parmananda Divarkar, SJ, (1995), 9. Institute of Jesuit Sources, St. Louis, 1995.

14. Rule 3, First Week, Puhl.

15. The publisher later changed the title to *God's Voice Within.*

16. Cal Newport, *Deep Work* (New York: Grand Central Publishing, 2016), 145–46.

17. Hervé Coathalem, for example, believes it is so rare as to have no practical use for us, while Karl Rahner believes it to be an ordinary and frequent experience. Quoted in Michael Ivens, SJ, *Understanding the Spiritual Exercises: Text and Commentary: A Handbook for Retreat Directors* (Wiltshire, England: Cromwell Press, 1998), 229.

18. Jules Toner, *A Commentary on Saint Ignatius's Rules for the Discernment of Spirits* (St. Louis: The Institute of Jesuit Sources, 1982), 291–313.

19. Coathalem says that because the experience is so rare, it "does not seem to have much practical utility." Quoted in Ivens, 229–38.

20. This definition is supported by Ivens, who does not insist that there be no source whatsoever but merely that "in relation with anything that might have been already happening, it is discontinuous and disproportionate" (230).

21. Fourteenth Annotation, Puhl.

22. Dr. Michael Major. This therapist is a friend of mine and this was mentioned in passing, not in print.

23. Puhl, Paragraph #175.

24. This seems to be why Ignatius warned against making a "hasty vow" in Annotation 14.

25. Paragraph Nine of the 1550 Formula, p. 13. *The Constitutions of the Society of Jesus and Their Complementary Norms*, The Institute of Jesuit Sources, St. Louis, 1996, page 13.

26. Fourteenth Annotation, Puhl.

27. For the rest of this chapter, I mostly write using spiritual direction as the model, but I'm quite sure that the reader will easily be able to adapt it to his or her work as pastoral counselor, confessor, and so on.

28. For the most part in this section, I use the terms *director* and *directee*. But I mean for these insights to apply to any mentor, counselor, or adviser relationship.

29. Rule 5, First Week, Puhl.

30. Rule 13, First Week, Puhl.

31. Rule 5, Second Week, Puhl.

32. Rule 1, Second Week, Puhl.

33. See my Innovative Idea #7.

34. Rule 7, First Week, Puhl.

35. Seventh Annotation, Puhl.

36. Note that I do not include "problem fixer" on this list. We directors must always be suspicious of our desires to fix the directee's problems. Usually, this is not our role. God is the primary problem fixer, then the directee. The director is a distant third.

37. Seventh Annotation, Puhl.

38. Rule 7, First Week, Puhl.

39. Rule 6, First Week, Puhl.

40. David Fleming, SJ, *Draw Me into Your Friendship: The Spiritual Exercises* (St. Louis, MO: Institute of Jesuit Sources, 1996), 257.

41. Levenkron, Steven. *Cutting: Understanding and Overcoming Self-Mutilation*, W.W. Norton & Company, 1998, page 179.

42. Rule 11, First Week, Puhl.

43. This example of isolating oneself is an interesting one because it reveals how important it is to know your directee well. For some people, isolating themselves is a healthy thing because it leads to periods of self-reflection. For others, however, it is a form of "checking out of life."

44. This metaphor is in reference to the Fourteenth Rule of the First Week: "Just as a captain and leader of an army in the field, pitching his camp and exploring the fortifications and defenses of a stronghold, attacks it at the weakest point, in the same way the enemy of human nature, roving about, looks in turn at all our theological, cardinal, and moral virtues; and where he finds us weakest and most in need for our eternal salvation, there he attacks us and attempts to take us."

45. Rule 5, First Week, Puhl.

46. Second Annotation, Puhl.

47. Rule 5, First Week, Puhl.

48. Rule 5, First Week, Puhl.

49. Rule 10, First Week, Puhl.

50. Rule 9, First Week, Puhl. Note that Ignatius teaches us that God *allows* us to experience desolation but never initiates desolation within us.

51. Rule 6, Second Week, Puhl.

52. Rule 5, Second Week, Puhl.

53. Rule 14, First Week, Puhl.

54. For a full description of this experience, see my Innovative Idea #10.

55. See Innovative Ideas #11 and #12.

56. Puhl translation, excerpted from Ignatian Spirituality.com.

57. I find this metaphor so disturbing to our contemporary sensibilities as to be unusable in our time. Jesuit spiritual writer David Fleming uses a different metaphor that perfectly reflects the point that Ignatius is trying to make in this Twelfth Rule: "The evil spirit often behaves like a spoiled child. If a person is firm with children, children give up petulant ways of acting. But if a person shows indulgence or weakness in any way, children are merciless in trying to get what they want, stomping their feet in defiance or wheedling their way into favor. So our tactics must include firmness in dealing with the evil spirit in our lives." Fleming, *Draw Me into Your Friendship*, page 257.

58. I find this metaphor so disturbing to our contemporary sensibilities as to be unusable in our time. Jesuit spiritual writer David Fleming uses a different metaphor that perfectly reflects the point that Ignatius is trying to make in this Twelfth Rule: "The evil spirit often behaves like a spoiled child. If a person is firm with children, children give up petulant ways of acting. But if a person shows indulgence or weakness in any way, children are merciless in trying to get what they want, stomping their feet in defiance or wheedling their way into favor. So our tactics must include firmness in dealing with the evil spirit in our lives." Fleming, *Draw Me into Your Friendship*, 257.

59. This rule applies to consolation without previous cause insofar as one accepts its broad definition: the spiritual experience wherein the intensity of consolation we experience is far out of proportion to the preceding cause.

60. See Thibodeaux, *God's Voice Within* (Chicago: Loyola Press, 2010), 171.

61. Puhl, paragraphs #169–189. Although Ignatian practitioners refer to this section as the "Rules for Election," the Puhl translation calls this section "Making a Choice of a Way of Life."

About the Author

Mark E. Thibodeaux, SJ, has been a Jesuit for more than thirty years. He has served as novice director, spiritual director, and high school campus minister. He is the author of four popular books on prayer and spirituality, including *God's Voice Within* and *Reimagining the Ignatian Examen.* He lives in New Orleans, Louisiana, where he serves as pastor of Holy Name of Jesus Church and School.

Also by Mark E. Thibodeaux, SJ

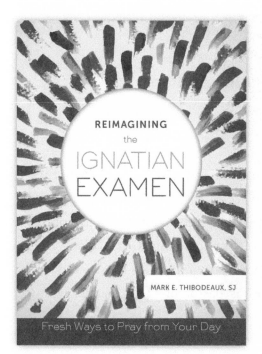

REIMAGINING THE IGNATIAN EXAMEN
FRESH WAYS TO PRAY FROM YOUR DAY

MARK E. THIBODEAUX, SJ

Join Mark E. Thibodeaux, SJ, as he guides you through new and unique versions of the Examen, totally flexible and adaptable to your life.

Reimagining the Ignatian Examen allows you to tailor your daily prayer practice to fit your personal and situational needs, further enhancing and deepening your meditation.

English: PB | 978-0-8294-4244-1 | $12.95
Spanish: PB | 978-0-8294-4512-1 | $12.95

DISCOVER THE **REIMAGINING THE EXAMEN** APP

Available for iOS and Android in English and Spanish, the **Reimagining the Examen app** allows you to take the tailor-made-reflections from *Reimagining the Ignatian Examen* on the go.

To Order:
Call **800.621.1008**, visit **store.loyolapress.com**, or visit your local bookseller.

Also by Mark E. Thibodeaux, SJ

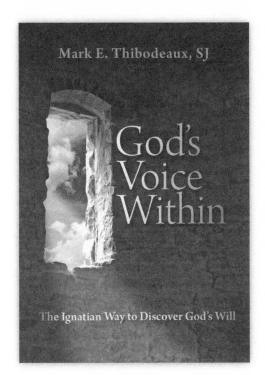

GOD'S VOICE WITHIN
THE IGNATIAN WAY TO DISCOVER GOD'S WILL

MARK E. THIBODEAUX, SJ

Foreword by James Martin, SJ

God's Voice Within is a spiritual resource for those who know that there is more to their spiritual life than they are currently experiencing and are ready to take the next step in their walk of faith.

This book guides readers as they develop their spiritual intuition, establish a practice of discernment, and respond to God's promptings within their hearts.

PB | 978-0-8294-2861-2 | $14.95